To Sue Bailey
Thank you for all these years of support. I will cherish them very much!
July/2022

Creativity in Management Education

"José-Rodrigo makes a timely and valuable contribution. Soft-tyrannies in management education seek better standardisation through ICT based assessments, more students and fewer educators and resources. To this, the author encourages us all to pursue our inner passions and embrace the spirit of play to rediscover creativity. This is not easy but essential for the future of business and humans".
—Professor Ziska Fields, *University of Johannesburg, South Africa*

"It is exciting that this book redefines creativity in management learning as seriously playful processes. The book deconstructs the current tyrannies of teaching management and injects a fresh spirit of creativity into it. Reading it will enable you to make sense of what is blocking your creative potential in the classroom, and see how you could explore new challenges and possibilities".
—Dr Tim Butcher, Associate Professor of Organisation Studies, *University of Tasmania (Australia)*

"It is a critical, moving and personal journey undertaken by the author, a testament to much needed resilience and creativity in our current educational systems".
—Dr Amanda Gregory, Senior Lecturer in Management Systems, *Hull University Business School, UK*

José-Rodrigo Córdoba-Pachón

Creativity in Management Education

A Systemic Rediscovery

palgrave
macmillan

José-Rodrigo Córdoba-Pachón
School of Business and Management
Royal Holloway, University of London
Egham, UK

ISBN 978-3-030-50959-0   ISBN 978-3-030-50960-6 (eBook)
https://doi.org/10.1007/978-3-030-50960-6

© The Editor(s) (if applicable) and The Author(s), under exclusive licence to Springer Nature Switzerland AG 2020
This work is subject to copyright. All rights are solely and exclusively licensed by the Publisher, whether the whole or part of the material is concerned, specifically the rights of translation, reprinting, reuse of illustrations, recitation, broadcasting, reproduction on microfilms or in any other physical way, and transmission or information storage and retrieval, electronic adaptation, computer software, or by similar or dissimilar methodology now known or hereafter developed.
The use of general descriptive names, registered names, trademarks, service marks, etc. in this publication does not imply, even in the absence of a specific statement, that such names are exempt from the relevant protective laws and regulations and therefore free for general use.
The publisher, the authors and the editors are safe to assume that the advice and information in this book are believed to be true and accurate at the date of publication. Neither the publisher nor the authors or the editors give a warranty, expressed or implied, with respect to the material contained herein or for any errors or omissions that may have been made. The publisher remains neutral with regard to jurisdictional claims in published maps and institutional affiliations.

Cover pattern © Melisa Hasan

This Palgrave Pivot imprint is published by the registered company Springer Nature Switzerland AG.
The registered company address is: Gewerbestrasse 11, 6330 Cham, Switzerland

*To my mother, an educational philosopher by heart, and always a noble soul.
God bless you.
And as you say: "No hay mal que por bien no venga".*

Acknowledgements

I would like to thank Francesca Robinson and Alice Lam from Royal Holloway, University of London (UK), and other university colleagues in the UK, France and Spain for letting me express and present my initial thoughts about this book, and encouraging me to pursue them further.

Would also like to thank my wife Cecilia and our twins (Sofi and Fabi), for letting me escape to cafes, the university library and the kitchen or living room to write. I am sorry for the many times I 'got lost in space'.

To Palgrave Macmillan (Srishti, Jessica, Vipin, Saif and colleagues) for all the support offered throughout.

To crises, and people supporting me through them. Let us not leave a good crisis to waste!

And to my students: Thank you for letting me be your educator, remember to keep your creativities alive!

Contents

1 **Introduction** 1
   Setting the Scene 1
   Structure of the Argument 5
   This Book in One Diagram 6
   Chapter Structure 6
   Conclusion 8
   References 8

2 **Soft Tyrannies for Creativity in Management Education** 11
   Introduction 11
   Soft Tyrannies: Programmes, Technologies, Emerging Functions 12
   Governing Programmes 15
      A Governing Programme: Education for Economic Growth 15
      A Governing Programme: Creativity Disciplining 16
   Governing Technologies 17
      Standardisation, Segmentations, Self and Moral Development 17
      Practice 18
      Assessment Technologies 19
   Emerging Power Functions 20
      The Creative Subject(s) 20
      Lack of Time 21
   Possibilities: (Self) Counter-Conducts 23
   Concluding Remarks 24
   References 24

3 Current Initiatives to Nurture Creativity   29
Introduction   29
Little c Creativity   30
Playing for Innovation   32
Inner Enthusiasm   34
Living a Creative Life   36
Learning to Learn   37
Learning by Interconnecting   39
Creative Schools   41
Reflections   42
Conclusion   44
References   44

4 A Systemic Space for Selves   47
Introduction   47
Traces of the Individual Self in Creativity and Applied Systems Thinking Research   48
  The 'I' in Creativity   48
  The 'System' and the Individual Selves   50
Revisiting Governmentality   53
Towards a Systemic Space for Individual, Creative Selves   57
Concluding Remarks   58
References   59

5 A Spirit of Play (and Seriousness)   63
Introduction   63
Play, Seriously?   64
Reclaiming Reflection Within Play   65
The Spirit of Childhood   67
  A Spirit for Play   68
  A Spirit of Seriousness   69
Implications for Enquiring About Creativity   71
  Life Stories   71
  Idea Biographies   71
Concluding Remarks   72
A Prelude   73
References   74

6	**First Rediscoveries of Creativity**	77
	Introduction	77
	The Alleyway	78
	(Type)writing	80
	The Lump(s)	82
	The University	84
	A Loss	87
	Exiting the Game: Serious Reflections	88
	Concluding Remarks	90
	References	91
7	**Taking Creativity to the Classroom**	93
	Introduction	93
	A game in Two Courts	94
	A Refreshing: Slowly (Re)recycling	95
	An Iteration: Recycling and Digital Innovation	97
	An Iteration: Diverging and Converging in Bike Recycling	98
	A Refreshing: (Re)learning About Numbers	99
	Iteration: Did We Fail?	102
	Iteration: Feedback and (Self) Compassion Arrive	104
	Time to Stop, Reflect and Be Serious Again	106
	Concluding Reflections	107
	References	108
8	**Summaries, Implications and Epilogue**	111
	Introduction	111
	The Argument Revisited	111
	Further Implications for the Rediscovery of Creativity	113
	A Brief Summary Guide to Play 'Rediscovering Creativity in Management Education'	115
	And an Epilogue	118
	References	119
	Index	121

About the Author

José-Rodrigo Córdoba-Pachón is an associate professor at the School of Business and Management, Royal Holloway, University of London. Prior to joining academia in the UK, he was a computer science and systems engineer, business and project manager and family entrepreneur in Colombia, his home country. He worked at organisations like Grexco Software and Fundación Social Group in Bogotá, Colombia, whilst also helping run a family business. After this, he obtained an MA (with distinction) and PhD in Management at the University of Hull. He was awarded an Economic and Social Research Council (ESRC) post-doctoral fellowship to establish his research in systems thinking. In 2003 he was nominated to the US Academy of Management William Newman Award for his best paper based on dissertation. He then joined the University of Hull as a lecturer in management systems and moved to Royal Holloway in 2008 as an associate professor, where he currently lectures in the undergraduate management programmes of the school, and leads educational initiatives at the digital innovation and management department (DIAM).

To date, José-Rodrigo has supervised to successful completion several PhD students in management, most of whom now also work in academia in the UK and elsewhere. José-Rodrigo's research on systems thinking is published in several articles in highly recognised international journals, monographs and edited books in English and Spanish. His previous single-authored books include *Systems Practice in the Information Society* (2010) and *Managing Creativity: A Systems Thinking Journey* (2019).

This present book is a contribution to management education using ideas from both systems thinking and creativity, as well as José-Rodrigo's experience as a student and management educator in the last 18 years.

List of Figures

Fig. 1.1	A feeling of old days	2
Fig. 1.2	Management Education Today	3
Fig. 1.3	This Book in One Diagram	4
Fig. 2.1	Governmentalities in management education	14
Fig. 2.2	Convergence of governing programmes and technologies	18
Fig. 3.1	Little c creativity	30
Fig. 3.2	Developing innovation in children	33
Fig. 3.3	A 'culture' system for innovation (inspired in Wagner)	34
Fig. 3.4	Learning how to learn	38
Fig. 3.5	A systemic paradox in nurturing creativity	43
Fig. 4.1	Selves, wholes and soft tyrannies	52
Fig. 4.2	A systemic space for selves	58
Fig. 6.1	A map of a hide and seek game	78
Fig. 6.2	A kindergarten picture	79
Fig. 6.3	Typewriter (s)	81
Fig. 6.4	The lump(s)	82
Fig. 7.1	Two courts of a new game	94
Fig. 7.2	(Re)learning about numbers	102

CHAPTER 1

Introduction

SETTING THE SCENE

Today, I am sitting in a large lecture theatre as an observer. I wait until everyone else leaves. My feelings of frustration as a student have resurfaced. I feel I am not capable to learn, let alone creative enough to put into practice what I have been lectured on. As a student, it might be tempting to take notes, check social media on my phone, or think of skipping the next sessions and doing nothing for this course.

I wonder if other classmates feel the same way, or how I would feel if I had to take over this course as a teacher.

I will have to learn about numbers and statistics again, teach in front of hundreds of students… **Where will be my creativity, their creativity, in all of this?**

This feeling and thoughts evoke memories of when I was an undergraduate engineering student many years ago. After a few semesters, I decided to *pass rather than fully learn* subjects like physics and later calculus, algebra, statistics and mathematical logic: I enjoyed other subjects like systems thinking, software programming or history and philosophy. The difference today is that I am (going to be) teaching many students. As an educator, I see myself as in a 'saving' mission to entice them to like what they are learning, to awaken their minds and nurture their creativity. My saviour and perfectionist-anxious selves surface again (Fig. 1.1).

Fortunately, I am now bit more mindful of my fears, and try not to berate myself too much. When that happens, I stop, rest and reflect.

© The Author(s) 2020
J.-R. Córdoba-Pachón, *Creativity in Management Education*,
https://doi.org/10.1007/978-3-030-50960-6_1

Fig. 1.1 A feeling of old days

Beyond me, there is an education system in management that influences all of us. And there is a perceived lack of time to reflect before acting, a paradox and a tension in our technology-mediated, Westernised societies worldwide (Rose 2013).

When I studied engineering in the late 1980s and early 1990s in Colombia, my home country, there were talks and meetings with students about making our curricula less mathematically driven and more oriented to consider technological solutions provided by (US-based) companies. Despite being initially inspired by American academia, our overall university curricula also paid attention to European research in informatics and systems thinking, developing awareness about our own country history and specific social problems. During my degree, I was able to take courses on history, social psychology, ethics and society.

And halfway through my five-year degree, *one day the penny dropped*, and it keeps doing so in my current job as a management educator: we need to challenge our assumptions about how we conceive of and nurture creativity in education. We need to continuously rediscover it for our benefit and that of our societies.

Many of my management students today seem to be wanting to have quick fixes or solutions to problems; many also say they enrolled in management, partly because they hate mathematics or numbers. They are impatient if they cannot see the impacts of their actions or their education (Wagner 2015). Students want to get high-flying jobs or set up their own (successful) business whereas others want to contribute to saving the planet. All with little time to consider several options when solving problems, asking us as educators to provide the 'right' answers or paths (Fig. 1.2).

As Fig. 1.2 also shows, in countries like the UK, there is pressure to strengthen data-driven, **numeracy skills** in management education, and link this with the use of *data analytics* solutions, many of which have been produced by globally known companies (SAS©, SAP©, etc.). There is also an imperative to educate our students to make them more aware of sustainability issues in contrast with a drive to only generate profits. And there is a drive to encourage students to be more entrepreneurial whilst also ensuring that they can fit into different types of organisations and cultural contexts.

As educators, we implicitly expect students to learn to live in an increasingly uncertain world, being able to reconcile tensions and sources of

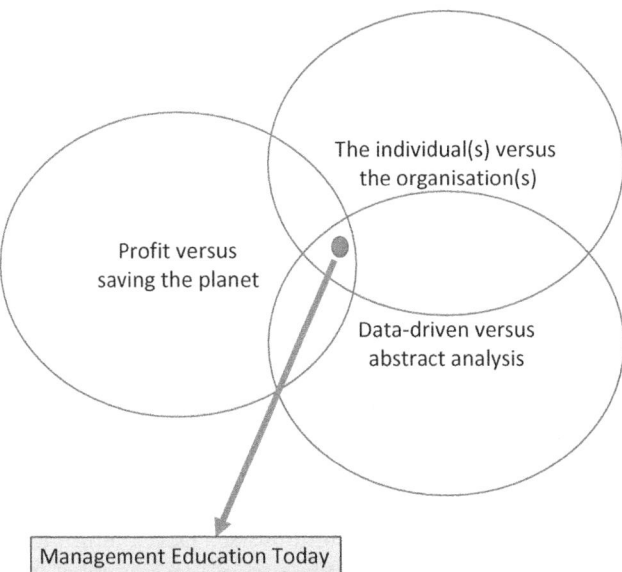

Fig. 1.2 Management Education Today

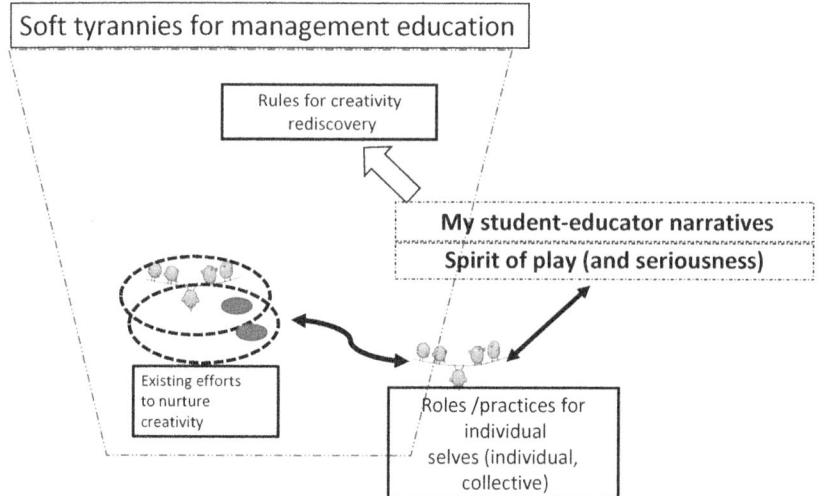

Fig. 1.3 This Book in One Diagram

knowledge (Abbott 1988). We ask them to come up with creative ideas that could have some degree of (commercial) application or benefit to others. Through promoting continuous collaboration and practically oriented learning, we currently assume that in this way we are contributing to make them more creative and innovative. Throwing them in at the deep end, we expect them to learn to swim and survive.

In this rush to the top, as educators we are failing to ask our students to formulate and address more personal and relevant questions for today's world: How about our curiosity and imagination? Are we being 'true' to ourselves? What could be the consequences of becoming creative as our societies want or need us to be?

As authors like Rose (2013) and Berg and Seeber (2016) concur, there is a need to *slow down* the pace of our higher education systems and *reflect* on what it means to be human. There might be a need to be solitary, pondering, introvert selves in our interactions with others that need to be rescued. Or there might be a need to transcend, with acceptance and humility, what we mean by the idea of a 'creative self' in relation to other living beings, our planet or even the universe. Developing ideas around these possibilities could require all of us to go back to what we used to enjoy as children (i.e. play), as well as taking the view that *the more* we try to normalise or standardise creativity in management education, *the less* we are helping our students become more creative. We also need to be serious to accept that which we cannot control and challenge what we think could change.

This book is an attempt to make better sense of what we mean by creativity in management education and provide some answers to the above tensions. It aims to help educators, students and other people involved or affected to appreciate the complex issues and dilemmas involved in the inclusion of 'other' forms of being or acting creatively, which could lead all of us to reflect on other ways of being ourselves. Whether we succeed in this attempt would depend on our willingness to stop and wonder, to play with ideas and imagine, to say no to some existing educational practices and to be more inclusive of other forms of thought or action.

Structure of the Argument

In this book I reconsider how as individuals we have become subjected to certain forms of nurturing creativity in management education. A critical analysis of how we have become creative subjects is undertaken to then lead to further reflections on what we consider a self to be and what we can do about it in playful, serious and power-aware ways.

Our educational organisations in management induce certain options for thinking and acting creatively at the expense of others, resulting in the operation of **soft tyrannies**. To coin this latter term, I have been influenced by the ideas of Michel Foucault on governmentality (1978, 1991, 1994), as well as my own conceptual work on critical systems thinking and the notion of the 'other' (Córdoba-Pachón 2002, 2019).

Soft tyrannies take the form of power programmes, technologies and functions that result in the formation of a creative subject. As Foucault (1994) says, existing forms of this subjectivation could be redefined or be done away with. This could be done in playful and serious ways and in consideration of power relations.

These tyrannies shape the type of creative subjects we aspire ourselves and our students to be with and in management education. Fortunately, there is scope for educators to think and act differently within these tyrannies and using our available freedom. I propose doing so by developing new ways of relating self and others and doing so by rediscovering the notion(s) of **play** (and seriousness) as a spirit (Droit 2018).

Through playful and serious narratives, I identify the (possible) presence of creativity with me and others becoming the players in different games. These lead me to formulate some rules of play that could be useful for students, educators and other relevant stakeholders if we want to continue rediscovering creativity within ourselves and in what we think or do.

THIS BOOK IN ONE DIAGRAM

As Fig. 1.3 shows (left, bottom, right, up), I first venture to identify soft tyrannies of power that shape creative subjects in management education. I then go on to review some efforts to nurture creativity in early and management education in order to identify potential contradictions that individual selves must deal with. With these grounds already covered, I then extend Foucault's ideas on governmentality to allow for individual or collective roles, practices (activities) and relationships in creativity, which could help us all to reconsider who we could become in management education. I then propose a spirit of play and seriousness to support this self-reflection. Using these ideas, I narrate my accounts (games) of being an engineering student and management educator to formulate game rules to help our systemic rediscovery of creativity in management education.

CHAPTER STRUCTURE

This first and introductory chapter provides an overview of the argument to be developed throughout the rest of the book. Chapter 2 provides a critical identification and analysis of soft tyrannies that operate the shaping of creative selves in management education. Following Foucault's ideas on governmentality, the operation of such tyrannies is denounced through the identification of power programmes, technologies and emerging functions. Some generic possibilities of counter-conduct are proposed.

Chapter 3 reviews some current approaches to the nurturing of creativity for management education. In the review, it is found that whilst many of these approaches highlight the importance of flexibility, and balance creativity with other forms of learning in educational systems via activities like play, there is an inherent *contradiction* or systemic paradox that needs to be addressed: creative individuals are considered as being already part of such systems or the universe as a whole, but they have to use their inner selves to become full members of them.

To address the above systemic contradiction/paradox, Chap. 4 presents critical ideas about self-others. I further draw on Foucault's ideas to contextualise and extend the scope of governmentality so that this notion can be used as an educational tool (Noguera 2009). With this possibility, a systemic space for individual selves to assume individual or collective roles and use some practices like reading, writing, mindfulness meditation or humouring is laid out. This space is likened to a 'house' that as educators we could inhabit with our students in order to rediscover our creativities or continue doing so.

With different roles and practices proposed for individual selves, Chap. 5 details Jean-Paul Droit (2018)'s ideas about **play**. Linking Western and Eastern thinking traditions, Droit's account of the spirit of childhood suggests that it is possible to transcend ideas about selves and others by adopting a spirit for play (and seriousness). This means that we could tame or deal with it by imagining, muting, repeating, refreshing-restarting it. It is in the emerging game iterations where we could find other forms of thinking, acting or being in the form of game rules. With a spirit of play, we could put ourselves in touch with the 'past', the 'present', or the 'timeless', allowing us to imagine other forms to interact with ourselves and others, thus offering us a source for creativity.

Alongside the spirit of playfulness, there is the spirit of seriousness. Creativity would need to stop to let reflection take place. In the face of so-called 'failure', this spirit could help us ground ourselves in the world as it is, encourage us to accept things as they are for our own sanity or sake and that of our loved ones (even if that means acknowledging the inevitability of some 'sh*t' in our lives). A more palatable paradox.

With the above ideas, Chap. 6 presents a reflective narrative of what I call a game of hide and seek with creativity. By (re)playing and narrating this game, I rediscover different selves of mine. In the game, I give creativity the role of a muse whose seeking has kept me enthusiastic and safe despite many unwanted collective roles. I read, write, meditate and reflect.

Chapter 7 speaks about another game termed 'let us protect our most precious selves'. In this game, with creativity now as my friend, we get to the management education classroom and use previously reviewed ideas to nurture creativity. We play in two courts (re-cycling and learning numbers). Among other things that happen in this game, I reflect on how we need to celebrate and value creativity when we feel it happens, and how we need to be aware of large courses teaching and student feedback. These could be curtailing possibilities to bring and live our best selves to our learning and lives in general. We need to say no for the benefit of ourselves and others.

In both Chaps. 6 and 7, I draw some game rules which could help my and others' selves continue rediscovering creativity in the light of soft tyrannies for management education. From these reflections, in Chap. 8, I round up the argument of this book with summaries, further implications for the systemic rediscovery of creativity and an epilogue.

Conclusion

This introductory chapter has laid out the main argument and structure of this book. The idea has been put forward that a rediscovery of creativity in management education requires us as educators and other stakeholders to take a step back and reflect on our ideas about ourselves and others. To address this issue, it is important first to better understand how management educational systems have shaped what we conceive of as creative subjects. In the next chapter of this book, an initial analysis of such systems is undertaken.

References

Abbott, A. (1988). *The System of Professions: An Essay on the Division of Expert Labour*. Chicago: The University of Chicago Press.

Berg, M., & Seeber, B. (2016). *The Slow Professor: Challenging the Culture of Speed in the Academy*. Toronto: University of Toronto Press.

Córdoba-Pachón, J.R. (2002). *A Critical Systems Thinking Approach for the Planning of Information Technology in the Information Society*. Unpublished PhD thesis. Hull: University of Hull.

Córdoba-Pachón, J. R. (2019). *Managing Creativity: A Systems Thinking Journey*. London: Routledge.

Droit, J. P. (2018). *Volver a ser Niño: Experiencias de Filosofía* (trans: Núria Petit Fontserè). Spain: Ediciones Paidós.

Foucault, M. (1978). Governmentality. In G. Burchell, C. Gordon, & P. Miller (Eds.), *The Foucault Effect: Studies in Governmentality* (pp. 87–104). Chicago: The University of Chicago Press.

Foucault, M. (1991). Questions of Method. In G. Burchell, C. Gordon&, & P. Miller (Eds.), *The Foucault Effect: Studies in Governmentality* (pp. 73–86). Chicago: The University of Chicago Press.

Foucault, M. (1994). The Ethics of the Concern for Self as a Practice of Freedom. In P. Rabinow (Ed.), *Michel Foucault: Ethics, Subjectivity and Truth* (pp. 281–302). London: Penguin.

Noguera, C. (2009). La Gubernamentalidad en Los Cursos del Profesor Foucault. *Educaçáo & Realidade, 34*(2), 21–33.

Rose, E. (2013). *On Reflection: An Essay on Technology, Education and the Status of Thought in the Twenty-First Century.* Toronto: Canadian Scholars' Press Inc.

Wagner, T. (2015). *Creating Innovators: The Making of Young People Who Will Change the World.* New York: Scribner, Simon and Schuster, Inc.

CHAPTER 2

Soft Tyrannies for Creativity in Management Education

INTRODUCTION

This chapter offers a detailed and critical analysis of how creativity, both as a phenomenon and as a domain of knowledge, is being dealt with in management education. A set of convergences including a dominant link between creativity and economic progress has fuelled our idea of what it means to be creative in management education.

As a result, we have creative subjects: **people with a specific script to become creative, and when doing so, with little time to reflect or doing anything else.** This situation arises because, far from being an imposition, this regulation continuously and softly 'nudges' us to align ourselves with it, under an overall idea that as **free individuals**, we are all contributing to the 'good' of society with our creativity (ies) and innovation(s).

As the reader can notice from this claim, the conceptualisation of this analysis is inspired by Foucault's ideas on governmentality, power and ethics (Foucault 1978, 1991, 2009; Gordon 1980, 1991; Lemke 2002; Dean 2009). I have used many of these ideas previously when analysing the issue of work-life balance in the pursuit of creativity (Córdoba-Pachón 2019). I now take them to provide an analytical glimpse of the educational environments where I normally work and want to rediscover creativity now. I also hope that as management educators we could become more aware and stop, think and live a bit more fully and critically than we

© The Author(s) 2020
J.-R. Córdoba-Pachón, *Creativity in Management Education*,
https://doi.org/10.1007/978-3-030-50960-6_2

currently do, reflecting this in our students and other stakeholders of our management educational systems.

The chapter begins by proposing three (3) elements of analysis: power programmes, technologies and functions, contributing to shape what we understand by creative subjects. I elicit them and their effects of their operation in my current management education practices. Further, I undertake a reflection to elicit what I call conduct and counter-conduct possibilities for the rediscovery of creativity in its ways of being, thinking and acting by educators, students and other stakeholders of management education.

Soft Tyrannies: Programmes, Technologies, Emerging Functions

Table 2.1 shows a diversity of definitions of creativity to date. Coming from different disciplines of knowledge, what seems to be common from the above manifestations is that they relate creativity mostly to individual selves with specific qualities, traits or motivations, and in interaction(s) with each other.

How these definitions emerge, both in theory or in practice, could be attributed to the operation of power relations in society, or what I call **soft tyrannies**. Drawing on Foucault and his work on governmentality (Foucault 1978, 1991; Gordon 1980, 1991; Lemke 2002; Rose, O'Malley and Valverde 2006; Noguera 2009; Foucault 2009; Dean 2009), it can be said that our social relations involve *the structuring or setting up of spaces of possibilities for creatively being, thinking and acting*, which we realise individually or collectively in our interactions with ourselves or others. These possibilities, inevitably, have to do with ensuring that society is (self) regulated.

'**Soft**' means that they are 'nudged upon' us as educators, students or other stakeholders involved or affected by them. They possibly emerged out of good intentions, presupposing ways of thinking and acting about 'being freely creative' (Foucault 1978; Gordon 1980, 1991; Rose et al. 2006). '**Tyrannies**' mean that for individuals there is some (little) space for manoeuvre or for thinking of other ways in which we could do otherwise.

In our Westernised societies and according to Foucault (1990), the last two centuries have brought to the fore the idea that we are to care for, if not govern, our 'bodies' (minds included) and that doing so is necessary for the welfare of our societies. We are to pursue the acquiring of knowledge on

Table 2.1 Some current definitions of creativity

'Discipline' or 'domain' of knowledge	What is creativity?
Psychology (Barron, 1968; Csikszentmihalyi 1988, 1996)	Developing or adapting oneself and ideas to one's own psychological traits, skills, expertise and environments, potentially resulting in discovering and addressing new problems and redefining / being shaped by existing domains and fields of knowledge.
Early education and psychology (Craft 2001)	Exploring, envisioning and acting on possibilities for positive self-adaptation and transformation in daily life situations and contexts, using self-efficacy or problem-solving capabilities.
Education (Oakley 2014; Wagner 2015; Robinson and Aronica 2016)	A process of discovering our purpose in life, supported by flexible and adaptive systems. Such systems should embed cultural processes of 'meme' transmissions that could help nurture students' curiosity and development of inner talents in interaction with relevant groups or audiences.
Literary writing (Pope 2005)	A plethora of *creativities*, imbricating humans and their available (cyborg) technologies, leading us to become critical about what or how we mean by a creative human self and others and how we research on creativity.
Dance choreography (Tharp 2002)	A life habit of bringing inspiration to life through continuous, routinely, ritual-based, performative, interactive, (self)-critical and (self)-honest work.
Science (Lehrer 2012)	Searching for and/or bringing together separate ideas or domains of knowledge; the result of borrowing, friction, gaining and refining between ourselves and others.
Innovation (Amabile 1998; Sawyer 2006; Andriopoulous and Dawson 2009)	A (systemic) process emerging from collaborative, 'organisational' or 'cluster' change tensions which also require appropriate identification and management of individual and collective skills, digital and privacy rights.
Artificial intelligence (Bostrom 2016; Tegmark 2018)	Modelling, generation of decisions in pre-defined 'spaces', together with patterns of association and using automatable and autonomous methods or techniques (i.e. machine-oriented learning)

how to do so. This knowledge (implicit or explicit in spoken language) is knowledge *in relation* to things, people and ways of relating to both (including relationships to oneself) (Foucault 1978). Knowledge operates as embedded in ways of thinking and acting, which include how we are to influence ourselves and others, to govern, to administer our conduct (Foucault 1978, 2009).

If we want to discern of 'other' (not structured) possibilities for thinking or acting within our available freedom in society, we could then identify several types of power relationships that we as individual or collective subjects are being subjected to, and which we could also influence with what we think is our available freedom. In this regard Rose et al. (2006, pp. 99–101, bold added) say:

> [Government power] is not assumed to be a by-product or necessary effect of immanent social or economic forces or structures. Rather, it is an attempt by those confronting certain social conditions to make sense of their environment, to imagine ways of improving the, and to devise ways of achieving these ends. **Human powers of creativity are centred rather than marginalized**, even though such creation takes place within certain styles of thought and must perforce make use of available resources, techniques, and so on.

The operation of soft tyrannies could involve different types of power relations. The following are proposed for analysis: **(a) Governing programmes; (b) Governing technologies associated to programmes; (c) Emerging power functions**. As shown in Fig. 2.1, their resulting operation brings about possibilities for conduct and counter-conduct for individual or collective subjects.

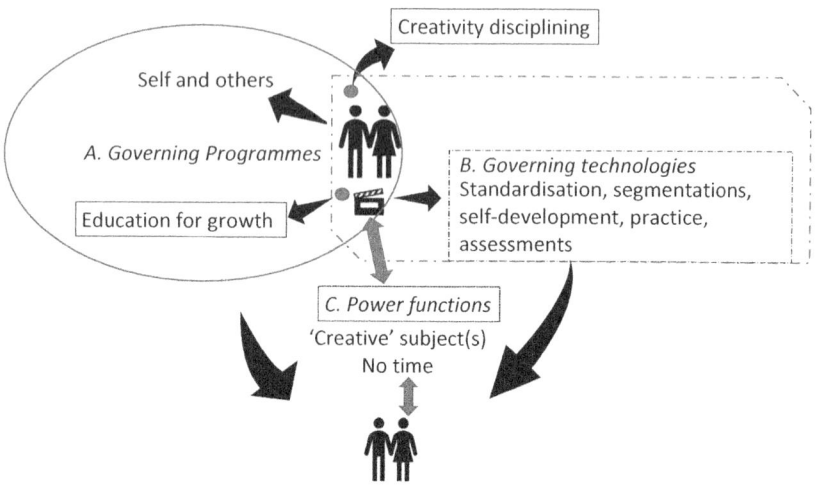

Fig. 2.1 Governmentalities in management education

Governing Programmes

In Foucault's work, governing programmes refer to 'visible' (language discourse-based) ways in which populations become conceived of in terms of declared needs and goals to fulfil (Foucault 1978, 2009; Gordon 1980; Kendall and Wickham 1999). Needs and goals are declared as they are defined, meaning that such definition is embedded in the operation of power relations that constitute individual or collective subjects (Gordon 1980). Declarations of goals and needs are followed by ways of thinking and acting that aim to meet them.

According to Foucault (1994), it is when some initially 'innocuous' but potentially disrupting events occur, leading to the establishment of certain objectivity of needs/goals, the development of a politics and a government of individual or collective selves, together with the elaboration of ethics and practices, that governing programmes are established.

A Governing Programme: Education for Economic Growth

A main governing programme that has influenced how we think and behave (rushing, dividing attention) is that of being educated for economic purposes. In the global realm of education, Robinson and Aronica (2016, pp. 9–10) highlight the features of this programme as consisting of:

> A high performing education system [or systems that] is [are] critical to national economic prosperity and to staying ahead of our [country] competitors. Standards of academic achievement must be as high as possible, and schools [among other institutions] must give priority to subjects and methods of teaching that promote these standards...it is essential that as many people as possible go on to higher education, especially four-year colleges and universities...government[s] need to take control of education by setting the standards, specifying the content of the curriculum, testing students systematically...and making education more efficient through increased accountability and competition.

The above programme now operates in what could be conceived of as 'natural', but there are disruptions. Some of these are currently more vocal and explicit, like for instance the student movements in Latin America or Hong Kong. Others are more subtle or now seen as 'normal', like recent academic strikes or earlier strikes regarding tuition fees in the UK. And many others are being disrupted by the global coronavirus situation and its aftermath. In all these events, the critical historian or analyst has an opportunity to identify the conditions that have led the present to become what it is (Gordon 1980), and suggest ways to creatively redefine it by deciding what is (not) necessary anymore for the constitution of selves as governable subjects.

This book is an attempt to call into question the existence of this governing programme as well as the following one. Their effects are denounced and some possibilities to counteract them as well as their associated governing power technologies and emerging functions proposed. This is with the aim of rediscovering creativity as a systemic space of redefinition of relationships between us and others in management education.

A Governing Programme: Creativity Disciplining

According to Runco and Albert (2010), the twentieth century brought with it several questions that still gather the interests of researchers in creativity. Questions like: *What is creativity, who has it, who can benefit from it, can it be increased through conscious effort?* have influenced our understandings of creativity as portrayed above, and how we (could) nurture it through research and practice.

The pursuit of answers to the above questions has also contributed to distinguish creativity as a socially legitimate and scientifically rigorous field of knowledge (Sternberg and Lubbart 1999; Pope 2005; Runco and Albert 2010). Currently, research in creativity is continuously characterised and progressed by courses, journals, journal articles, single or edited books (including this one), and conferences. Furthermore, three key elements seem to maintain it. Firstly, there are several **individual tests** that can be used to assess it at both the individual and collective level (the latter can overlap with the field of innovation). Secondly, there are **generic criteria** to assess creativity of a process, idea or a product. Criteria such as *novelty, value to others than the creators themselves and something that 'works'* (Sternberg and Lubbart 1999; Pope 2005; Runco and Jaeger 2012; Cropley and Cropley 2016). And thirdly, there are now a series of socio-cultural **principles** that aim to inform future developments in the field (Glavenau et al. 2019). Among those principles, the economic, psychological, cultural and social importance of creativity is highlighted, together with ways in which such importance is to be brought forth (Montuori and Purser 1995; Glavenau 2010).

These and other developments in the creativity field suggest that it is becoming more structured, recognised and disciplined, as newcomers to it need to 'know' and act accordingly. Developments, however, could also limit the conduct of people enquiring, researching about or teaching/learning creativity, as well as of those who want to become creative.

Governing Technologies

According to Foucault (1991), for governing programmes to meet their declared objectives, it is necessary to design or make available **governing technologies of power** (Foucault, 1978, 1988, 1991, 2009).

These can be defined as procedures, scripts, 'algorithms' or norms that establish gaps between objectives and forms of human conduct, as well as ways to close them (Gordon 1980, 1991; Kendall and Wickham 1999). Governing technologies help constitute and operate power relations by (re)defining them in terms of who controls whom, by which means or procedures (often innocuous or just taken for granted), and for which purposes (normally although not necessarily aligned to governing programme objectives).

The above governing technologies are diverse. They include for instance those that ensure the population's compliance with norms (i.e. surveillance, structuring of spaces and behaviours), as well as those that people use to *work on themselves* to also ensure compliance with a vision of the type of 'subject' they 'want' to be or become. In their operation, governing technologies can use information and communication technologies or ICTs to gather statistical knowledge about populations, implementing also activities of (self) education, monitoring, profiling, assembling, compliance and punishment (Foucault 1988; Rose et al. 2006). Moreover, through the operation of governing technologies, people's conduct can also be *revealed*, and thus adjusted accordingly by those governing them or by people themselves. Hence the importance of knowledge in our societies to better understand and manage ourselves and others.

Standardisation, Segmentations, Self and Moral Development

In management education, standardisation constitutes a current and very influential way by which the above government programmes become implemented. Standardisation of education and its associated practices has helped to increase the scale and scope of management programmes. Alongside standardisation, categorisation of types of creativity that could be identified from individuals (Craft 2001; Kaufman and Beghetto 2009; Hanson 2013) helps to fill existing gaps of creativity understanding, education and acting.

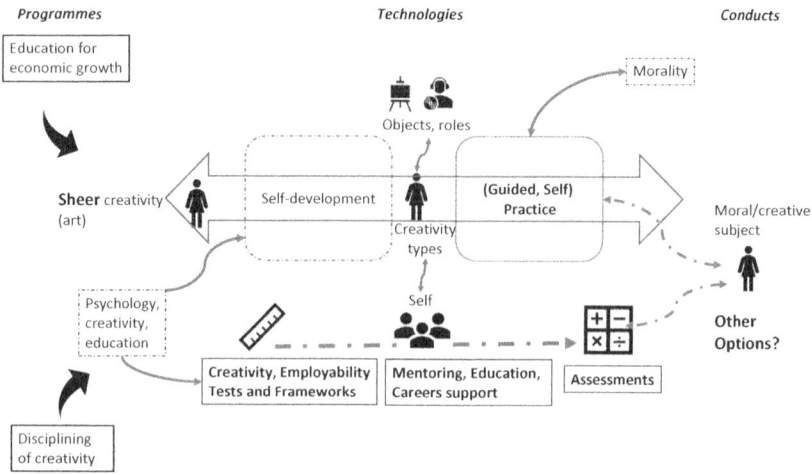

Fig. 2.2 Convergence of governing programmes and technologies

From 'little' to 'big' creativity types, an enabler of their categorisations or transitions between them is the notion of 'self-development/efficacy' (Craft 2001), which could lead individuals to identify where they are at and decide where to go next. This can potentially generate the idea of a creative process as progressive and linear as portrayed in Fig. 2.2. Self-development/efficacy is linked to other ideas like 'intentional' and 'moral development' (Gruber 1993; Runco and Nemiro 2003), which could contribute to reinforce the idea that creative subjects need to '*morally grow*' or '*develop*', and thus exert ways of conducting themselves (i.e. by practising their learning), in order to be considered as such, or succeed in their creative efforts.

Practice

As shown with the different definitions about creativity at the beginning of this chapter, there is a strong relationship between creativity and practice. For instance, Wagner (2015) acknowledges that creative individuals have a positive outlook about situations, 'a belief that through trial and error a deeper understanding and better approaches [to solve problems] can be discovered' (p. 15, brackets added). This also relates to what Wagner advocates as a design thinking mentality, in which failure is considered just another iteration in learning towards succeeding, and where nothing in our world stays the same. In addition, Csikszentmihalyi (1988, 1996) considers that individuals first need to learn (by trial and error, in other words failure) the specifics of a domain of knowledge in order to be able to generate something novel within it.

Other authors like Sternberg and Kaufmann (2010) and Oakley (2014) identify different types of cognitive processes that assume that individuals immerse themselves in trying and failing in their creative journeys (i.e. selective encoding, combination, comparison, focusing or diffusing). Lehrer (2012) also considers how individuals who master one or several domains of knowledge can then generate creativity by integrating their previous knowledge into a new domain, and Tharp (2002) highlights routines/habits (i.e. having a box to think outside of the box, rituals) to help creators shape and test their ideas.

What transpires from these and other takes is an inherited assumption that practice is to be made *iterative, explicit or rationally/morally managed* mainly by individuals themselves (possibly with the help of tutors, mentors or work groups). However, it is them who are responsible for carrying it out to attribute meaning, to then *reveal* its results or outcomes to (educators) audiences, transforming themselves in the process, and assume the consequences of their practice.

Whilst practice could be considered an essential attribute of human learning, what seems to be lacking in creativity education is the need for creators to take a step back (i.e. by failing or just stopping) and reflect on *the type of creative subject* that is emerging as a result of practicing, so that they can decide to pursue it or be/do otherwise) via different (not only structured or planned) practices or roles. In this regard, links between practice, reflection and failure in creativity education are yet to be fully understood as part of systemic creative processes and situations, some of which might inhibit rather than nurture creativity (Hanson 2013).

Assessment Technologies

Figure 2.2 also shows how the convergence of standardisation, self-development notions and practice could be monitored or corrected via assessment technologies. Among others, the proposed creativity assessment frameworks of Cropley and Cropley (2000, 2016) and Pefanis-Schlee and Harich (2014) in education assume that it is *necessary and desirable* to 'test educational' subjects (individually or in groups) on their creative abilities or traits (i.e. boundary challenging, unconventionality, metaphorical or prospective thinking, incubation of ideas, originality, flow, perspective-taking), *to then* provide some sort of 'corrective' support (creativity training, lecturing, mentoring) and *to then* assess them in relation to their performance or gaining of knowledge or skills.

And also with the (post) coronavirus situation, all of this can be made more efficient or immediate via online, information and communication technologies or ICTs, potentially generating a perceived lack of time for solitary, slow, non-purposeful but meaningful reflection that is currently and badly needed to nurture our individual and collective creativity (Rose 2013; Berg and Seeber 2016).

Emerging Power Functions

For Foucault (1978, 1991; Gordon 1980, 1991), the operation of governmentalities also generates certain and emerging functions that some actors within networks of power perform in order to meet specific objectives. Such objectives might not be necessarily aligned or like those explicitly declared by governing programmes. A critical historian could identify and elicit such functions in order to raise awareness about their consequences for the freedom of individual or collective subjects, and thus show possibilities for subjects to counteract them.

The Creative Subject(s)

A result of the above is that a type of creative subject is emerging from management education: one supposedly being highly sought and valued by employers worldwide. According to Wagner (2015, p. 16), the essential qualities of this subject are:

(i) Curiosity, which is a habit of asking good questions and a desire to understand more deeply.
(ii) Collaboration, which begins with listening to and learning from others who have perspectives and expertise that are very different from one's own.
(iii) Associative or integrative thinking.
(iv) A bias towards action and experimentation.

The shaping of this creative subject also affects educators. Under the above image of and assumptions about practising creators, I myself have been able to create my own power function by taking on several courses (i.e. quantitative methods, digital innovation and a creative process management course); I have been able to author several publications on systems thinking and creativity; students have been able to complete their degrees. As an educator in management, I feel that I need to continue learning new things so that I can instil them in my students. In my courses, I have promoted the importance of acknowledging paced and reflective practice, self-assessment and failure (Oakley 2014). Although some students value self-assessment as a way of preparing themselves for summative testing, sadly, not many seem to link practice (structured or unstructured) with reflections on what makes them *curious or passionate in life* (Wagner 2015). This and other insights will be later discussed in the book.

For now, it seems that the pressures of employability and 'economic debt' in management education (students nowadays take a loan to pay for their tuition fees and other expenses) could push people to focus on passing or obtaining good results at the expense of everything else. However, not all of us are to 'succeed'. Only 20% of the 20% of students that graduate in countries like the US or elsewhere end up working in career-related jobs with top salaries (Dobelli 2013; Wagner 2015). In this regard, Wagner (2015) also claims that of those individuals that work in career-related jobs, many end up following very similar paths, in other words, going for similar jobs at companies that are considered the 'elite'. A not very creative result!

A similar claim can be levelled for management educators: Academic structures of different institutions end up resembling each other, in order to facilitate staff mobility and homogeneity in the knowledge that is both transmitted to students and rediscovered via disciplinary competition (Abbot 2001). Although one could consider that the above managing of creative conduct in management education is necessary for the regulation of societies (Foucault 1994), a by-product that needs to be critically addressed is that for institutions, educators and students, creativity education is currently generating a limiting set of options, career paths and outcomes in our societies.

Lack of Time

A good number of my undergraduate management students in the UK—mostly in their late teens and early twenties—spend their time looking after their appearance, working part or full time, chatting with friends, attending family gatherings, checking their social media before or during class if not missing them. Without sounding too patronising with this observation, there seems to be no time for anything else. Myself, I strive to effectively manage my time between university and fatherhood, let alone be creative about my own well-being and at work (Córdoba-Pachón 2019). Teaching or learning, preparing for them, seeking funding opportunities, reading or writing, meeting students formally or informally, chatting to colleagues in the corridor or in a café, hosting visiting researchers, all of this whilst keeping a healthy body and mind (i.e. doing mindfulness meditation).

It takes time and encouragement for all of us to change 'the academic routine', for instance, to take things slowly and talk about it as genuine human beings (Berg and Seeber 2016), or to spend some time in individual solitude and reflection (Rose 2013). It takes courage for me not to be checking email, to spend time walking around a park, reading something that does not have anything to do with my research interests, to not think about work, promotion, collaboration or funding when I am with my close family, or to laugh at how serious I am. I can notice mine or other people's anxiety rising when things take a different course in our daily lives. I can also see anxiety in my students. We all seem to be running around with no end in sight.

As Ackoff and Rovin (2005) claim, with educational systems as they currently operate, we could be educating students to just get a job in which their 'real' learning will really kick-off, with a net effect that only some educators are able to reap benefits within the whole educational systems that have been set up. Ackoff and Rovin (2005) say:

> The principal [emerging power] function of a university is to provide its faculty members with the quality of work life and standard of living they want. Teaching is the price they must pay, and like any price, they try to minimize it [to have time for 'other' things, but what are they?]. The more distinguished faculty members, the less teaching it requires of its faculty… Tenure, clearly, is no longer primarily a way of protecting academic freedom, its espoused function, but [also] a way of protecting *incompetence*. (2005, pp. 19–20, brackets and italics added)

Using the power function of not having enough time, I sometimes have been able to make 'rushed' decisions towards achieving a 'better' work-life balance including taking some time to look after myself during working weeks (Córdoba-Pachón 2019) or writing books like this. But I still experience important dilemmas. I keep asking myself: is 'saying no' all there is in the pursuit of creativity nowadays? What about myself, the one who needs to be (un) creative at times to keep my own sanity and that of students or people around me?

Possibilities: (Self) Counter-Conducts

To the above consequences and dilemmas about creativity in management education, it becomes necessary to propose 'other' forms of operating within the skeleton of power relations for creativity education presented above. Like the above personal reflections, it might be time to let go of the imperatives of economic growth and no time, or at least loosen their grip over us, by addressing what we could consider the main ethic-political danger that we face in our societies (Foucault 1982), and by enabling people to address them within existing power relations as a way to exert our available freedom (Foucault 1984a, b, 1991, 1994). Some generic possibilities for (self) counter-conduct are proposed as follows.

Firstly, creativity as a phenomenon and as a field of knowledge could be considered as non-essential in societies. If its promotion is excluding other ways of thinking or acting, we as educators might *not need* to continue pushing for its establishment within the landscape of social science knowledge, or if doing so, we would need to *establish new objectives for it*. As mentioned before, there might be no need to explicitly link creativity with economic growth via the current shaping of creative subjects in education, or advance creativity knowledge for its own sake. There could be other forms of being (un) creative.

Secondly, existing governing technologies of standardisation, categorisation or self-development could be redirected to enable diverse and **process-based** interactions between management education stakeholders, and with a view that (information) technologies' monitoring role could be shifted towards better (self) understandings or interactions. Management educators and students could be allowed to exert their creativity in co-creating assessments, in taking them forward to practice-based contexts and reflecting on their insights (i.e. critical problem-based learning), inventing their own assessments or even not being assessed at all!

A key challenge for educational systems and institutions is to allow the above or other learning and assessment options to flourish and still be able to regulate our and students' conducts.

Thirdly, it becomes important to go deeper in enabling self-reflection in management education, so that the ingrained discourses, mentalities or technologies of conditional practice for creativity could be challenged. In his historical analyses of sexuality and the operation of power over ourselves (Foucault 1984a, 1990), Foucault shows how it was possible—and within the grids of practice made available by power relations—to be or *become someone else* than who was expected to be at the time.

Foucault did not aim to 'normalise' the above possibility or any historically emergent way of being or thinking (i.e. humanism). Rather, his aim was to encourage us to see that it is still possible to do so as a way of living in our present times. In this book, we first take up this possibility to explore in more depth how we could become different selves with creativity and its nurturing or rediscovery in management education. From the reflections gathered throughout the book, it would then be possible to ascertain more clearly the first and second possibilities for (self) counter-conduct at the end of it, providing some specific guidance to help us all 'play the games' of creativity rediscovery in management education.

Concluding Remarks

In this chapter, a first and critical glimpse of management education has been provided. Michel Foucault's ideas on governmentality have been used, to reveal how the unfolding of creativity in education is contributing to feed and reinforce images of creative subjects that fit within broader economic and knowledge disciplining purposes, and thus narrowing our thinking and acting about it.

To address this situation, some generic possibilities for (self) counter-conduct have been put forward. These possibilities are to be refined later by exploring in more detail how the nurturing of creativity continues resurfacing in education (next chapter of the book), and how we could provide more in-depth insights about our ideas about ourselves and others in management education.

References

Abbot, A. (2001). *Chaos of Disciplines*. Chicago: Chicago University Press.
Ackoff, R. L., & Rovin, S. (2005). *Beating the System: Using Creativity to Outsmart Bureaucracies*. San Francisco: Berrett-Koehler Publishers.
Amabile, T. (1998, September–October). How to Kill Creativity. *Harvard Business Review, 1998*, 77–87.
Andriopoulous, C., & Dawson, P. (2009). *Managing Creativity, Innovation and Change*. London: Financial Times/Prentice Hall.
Barron, F. (1968). *Creativity and Personal Freedom*. London: D. Van Nostrand Company Inc.
Berg, M., & Seeber, B. (2016). *The Slow Professor: Challenging the Culture of Speed in the Academy*. Toronto: University of Toronto Press.

Bostrom, N. (2016). *Superintelligence: Paths, Dangers, Strategies.* Oxford, UK: Oxford University Press.
Córdoba-Pachón, J. R. (2019). *Managing Creativity: A Systems Thinking Journey.* London: Routledge.
Craft, A. (2001). Little c Creativity. In A. Craft, B. Jeffrey, & M. Leibling (Eds.), *Creativity in Education* (pp. 45–51). London: Continuum.
Cropley, D., & Cropley, A. (2000). Fostering Creativity in Engineering Graduates. *High Ability Studies, 11*(2), 207–219.
Cropley, D., & Cropley, A. (2016). Promoting Creativity Through Assessment: A Formative Computer-Assisted Assessment Tool for Teachers. *Educational Technology, 56*(6), 17–24.
Csikszentmihalyi, M. (1988). Society, Culture and Person: A Systems View of Creativity. In M. Csikszentmihalyi (Ed.), *The Systems Model of Creativity: The Collected Works of Mihaly Csikszentmihalyi* (pp. 47–61). Dordrecht: Springer.
Csikszentmihalyi, M. (1996). *Creativity: Flow and the psychology of discovery and invention.* New York: Harper Collins.
Dean, M. (2009). *Governmentality: Power and Rule in Modern Society* (2nd ed.). London: Sage Publications Ltd.
Dean, M. (2010). *Governmentality: Power and Rule in Modern Society* (2nd ed.). London: Sage.
Dobelli, R. (2013). *The Art of Thinking Clearly.* London: Sceptre.
Foucault, M. (1978). Governmentality. In G. Burchell, C. Gordon, & P. Miller (Eds.), *The Foucault Effect: Studies in Governmentality* (pp. 87–104). Chicago: The University of Chicago Press.
Foucault, M. (1982). The Subject and Power. *Critical Inquiry, 8,* 777–795.
Foucault, M. (1984a). What is enlightenment? In P. Rabinow (Ed.), *The Foucault Reader: An Introduction to Foucault's Thought* (pp. 32–50). London: Penguin.
Foucault, M. (1984b). Polemics, Politics and Problematizations: An interview with Michel Foucault. In P. Rabinow (Ed.), *The Foucault reader: An introduction to Foucault's thought* (pp. 381–390). London: Penguin.
Foucault, M. (1988). Tecnologías del yo (Technologies of the Self). In M. Morey (Ed.), *Tecnologías del Yo y Otros Textos Afines* (pp. 45–94). Barcelona: Ediciones Paidós.
Foucault, M. (1990). *The Will to Knowledge: The History of Sexuality Volume 1.* Translated from French by Robert Hurley. London: Penguin.
Foucault, M. (1991). Questions of Method. In G. Burchell, C. Gordon, & P. Miller (Eds.), *The Foucault Effect: Studies in Governmentality* (pp. 73–86). Chicago: The University of Chicago Press.
Foucault, M. (1994). The Ethics of the Concern for Self as a Practice of Freedom. In P. Rabinow (Ed.), *Michel Foucault: Ethics, Subjectivity and Truth* (pp. 281–302). London: Penguin.
Foucault, M. (2009). *Security, Territory, Population.* London: Palgrave Macmillan.

Glavenau, V. (2010). Principles for a Cultural Psychology of Creativity. *Culture & Psychology, 16*(2), 147–163. https://doi.org/10.1177/1354067X10361394.

Glavenau, V., Hanson, M. H., Baer, J., Clapp, E., et al. (2019). Advancing Creativity Theory and Research: A Socio-Cultural Manifesto. *The Journal of Creative Behaviour, 0*(0), 1–5. https://doi.org/10.1002/jobc.395.

Gordon, C. (1980). Afterword. In C. Gordon (Ed.), *Michel Foucault: Power/Knowledge – Selected Interviews and Other Writings* (pp. 229–259). New York: Pantheon Books.

Gordon, C. (1991). Governmental Rationality: An Introduction. In G. Burchell, C. Gordon, & P. Miller (Eds.), *The Foucault Effect: Studies in Governmentality* (pp. 1–51). Chicago: The University of Chicago Press.

Gruber, H. (1993). Creativity in the Moral Domain: Ought Implies Can Implies Create. *Creativity Research Journal, 6*(1–2), 3–15.

Hanson, M. H. (2013). Author, Self, Monster: Using Foucault to Examine Functions of Creativity. *Journal of Theoretical and Psychological Psychology, 33*(1), 18–31.

Kaufman, J., & Beghetto, R. (2009). Beyond Big and Little: The Four C Model of Creativity. *Review of General Psychology, 13*(1), 1–12.

Kendall, G., & Wickham, G. (1999). *Using Foucault's Methods.* London: Sage Publications Ltd.

Lehrer, J. (2012). *Imagine: How Creativity Works.* New York: Houghton Mifflin Harcourt.

Lemke, T. (2002). Foucault, Governmentality and Critique. *Rethinking Marxism, 14*(3), 49–64. https://doi.org/10.180/089356902101242288, accessed July 2020.

Montuori, A., & Purser, R. (1995). Deconstructing the Lone Genius Myth: Toward a Contextual View of Creativity. *Journal of Humanistic Psychology, 35*(3), 69–112.

Noguera, C. (2009). La Gubernamentalidad en Los Cursos del Profesor Foucault. *Educação & Realidade, 34*(2), 21–33.

Oakley, B. (2014). *A Mind for Numbers.* Tarcher/Putnam: New York.

Pefanis-Schlee, R., & Harich, K. (2014). Teaching Creativity to Business Students: How Well Are We Doing? *Journal of Education for Business, 89*(3), 133–141.

Robinson, K. and Aronica, L. (2016). *Creative Schools.* New York: Penguin.

Pope, R. (2005). *Creativity: History, Theory, Practice.* Abingdon: Routledge.

Rose, E. (2013). *On Reflection: An Essay on Technology, Education and the Status of Thought in the Twenty-First Century.* Toronto: Canadian Scholars' Press.

Rose, N., O'Malley, P., & Valverde, M. (2006). Governmentality. *Annual Review of Law and Social Sciences, 2*, 83–104.

Runco, M., & Albert, R. (2010). Creativity Research: A Historical Review. In J. Kaufman & R. Sternberg (Eds.), *Handbook of Creativity* (pp. 3–19). Cambridge: Cambridge University Press.

Runco, M., & Jaeger, G. (2012). The Standard Definition of Creativity. *Creativity Research Journal, 24*(1), 92–96.

Runco, M., & Nemiro, J. (2003). Creativity in the Moral Domain: Integration and Implications. *Creativity Research Journal, 15*(1), 91–105.

Sawyer, K. (2006). *Explaining Creativity: The Science of Human Innovation.* Oxford: Oxford University Press.

Sternberg, R., & Kaufmann, J. (2010). Constraints on Creativity – Obvious and Not so Obvious. In J. Kaufman & R. Sternberg (Eds.), *Handbook of creativity* (pp. 467–482). Cambridge: Cambridge University Press.

Sternberg, R., & Lubbart, T. (1999). The Concept of Creativity: Prospects and Paradigms. In R. Sternberg (Ed.), *Handbook of Creativity* (pp. 3–15). Cambridge: Cambridge University Press.

Tegmark, M. (2018). *Life 3.0: Being Human in the Age of Artificial Intelligence.* London: Penguin Random House.

Tharp, T. (2002). *The Creative Habit: Learn It and Use It for Life.* New York: Simon and Schuster.

Wagner, T. (2015). *Creating Innovators: The Making of Young People Who Will Change the World.* New York: Scribner, Simon and Schuster.

CHAPTER 3

Current Initiatives to Nurture Creativity

INTRODUCTION

The previous chapter has identified the operation of key soft tyrannies in which creativity in management education is currently embedded. In the form of shaping creative subjects who have little time, it was argued that this operation could result in limited choices for individuals (academics, students, other stakeholders) to be or do 'otherwise' than expected.

Whether we like them or not, tyrannies and their operational power skeleton are here to stay or unfold, and we are part of them. However, as 'free', individual or collective subjects, we can use available freedom to shape ourselves and our students as 'other' types of people. Generic possibilities were offered to that end in the previous chapter of this book, whilst educators like me could continue our analytical quest to detail them. In doing so, we can also rediscover ourselves and our relationships with others (human and non-human).

In this chapter, a review of some of these current efforts to nurture creativity in education is conducted. There are several initiatives or efforts to nurture creativity that aim to diversify, make things slow and personalised for people, help us pursue our curiosity, interests and passions, and with a view of also nurturing creativity in our lives (Bateson 1994; Craft 2001; Oakley 2014; Wagner 2015; Robinson and Aronica 2016; Stern 2018).

The review leads to the identification of an inherent systemic paradox for creative individuals (students, educators, others): to already be part of 'wholes' whilst still developing themselves to gain full membership of them through creativity. This paradox will need to be further explored to continue refining counter-conduct possibilities for individual selves in our rediscovery of creativity in management education.

In the following sections, initiatives to nurture creativity in education are presented and assessed. Some of them put emphasis on the individual as a focus of creativity, whereas others also consider environmental factors (cultural, social) and even challenge the inherent value of creativity attributed by us and our societies.

LITTLE C CREATIVITY

The educator and researcher Anna Craft (2001) coins the term **little c creativity or LCC,** to account for a synergy between different individual traits (i.e. self-determination, conscious risk-taking, imagination, etc.) and desires, which could help people move on in their efforts to effect change in themselves and their environments.

Craft (2001) argues that LCC can be nurtured from an early age. Children could be (self) motivated to become open to pose imaginative questions and **play** with possibilities.

Figure 3.1 separates elements of LCC into the individual and the collectively oriented. This is because acts of LCC necessarily involve being in a **relationship** with someone, something or both, in order to direct or be

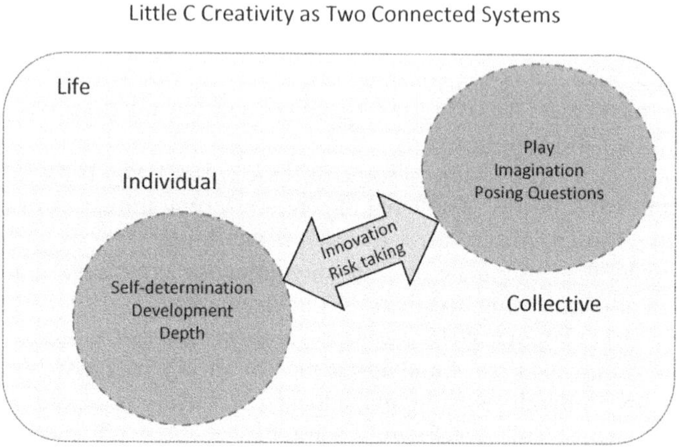

Fig. 3.1 Little c creativity

directed in one's quest for self-development, a kind of inner energy (also called self-efficacy or determination) that is essential to develop creativity, and doing so in relation to circumstances. As Craft (2001) says: 'One cannot be creative with respect to nothing' (p. 65). The relational nature of LCC implies several environmental challenges for individual educators and students. LCC requires active and intentional engagement with situations that pose challenges for individuals, using one's imagination, (possibility) thinking and drive to act.

With the above and drawing on the work of Mihaly Csikszentmihalyi (1988) and Howard Gardner (2011), Craft (2001) argues that knowledge can be found in diverse domains of life (Craft 2001, p. 56). With this, she also grounds creativity in *mundane* manifestations. LCC can be used in a variety of situations: from coping with everyday issues to transforming one's own conditions (i.e. life or career options), to embedding further abilities and knowledge to formulate questions (what if) and find solutions under the 'can do' belief.

Like Csikszentmihalyi's systems model of creativity (1988), LCC involves agents, cognitive processes (i.e. diverging, converging, problem finding/solving, imagining) and their domains of application. In making creativity happen, it is agents who can formulate and pursue goals. This means that their effective agency (i.e. self-development or self-efficacy) is at the centre of any creative effort. As individuals, we would all need to become empowered to meet new ideas with encouragement and support; to be able to interact with others, find information, tolerate uncertainty, take risks and own the consequences of our actions (Craft 2003).

However, LCC unfolding is not free of tensions or dilemmas according to Craft (2003), who highlights the confusion of terminology about creativity in education, how creativity is delivered (as a cross-course skill versus a separate subject) and the consequences of such modes of delivery, including the using of creativity as a political form of resistance against educational curricula centralisation or standardisation. Moreover, it could well be that in some cultural (authoritarian) contexts, situations or specific individual conditions (i.e. depression, anxiety, lack of motivation), developing inner energy or self-determination is difficult to achieve, or if it is achieved, there could be unforseen negative implications for individuals (i.e. burnouts caused by excessive dependence on previous successes or setbacks, lack of personal control). In this regard, LCC would need to emphasise a bit more how to better understand and deal with 'failure' in relation to the context or situation experienced, and how appropriate reflection and support could help individuals.

For educators, addressing these and other tensions would require a shift of roles and identities about ourselves, as well as questioning the inherent value given to creativity/failure for our lives and the lives of who we educate (Craft 2003). We need to challenge assumptions about if or how nurturing forms of creativity like LCC would *linearly* lead to individually or societally impactful forms, and for what purposes and with what consequences (Craft 2003).

Whilst Craft (2003) seems to encourage educators to find the right balance between promoting and resisting creativity education, my interpretation of it is that she is also encouraging us, students and potentially everyone else to *reflect on or reconsider who we are* and find ways of *becoming who we think we can be*, going beyond what we all consider to be our sense of selves. This would not mean renouncing the power we have within soft tyrannies for creativity education. Rather, it would mean becoming conscious of who we were/are and using this in meaningful ways to help ourselves and others.

Playing for Innovation

Tony Wagner (2015) aims to reconsider the importance of innovation in societies, and how we as educators could contribute to better nurture it. He traces back success in innovation to unstructured play in children, which he argues awakes curiosity and imagination, and later could fuel the discovery of passion and purpose, these ingredients being essential to sustain innovators in their quest to make a difference in the world.

Figure 3.2 shows how, through play, children (and adults) can venture in imagining possibilities as well as making them happen in the 'real' world; later, they can tune into what makes them passionate, fuelling also their inner motivations and sense of purpose(s).

For Wagner (2015), play as an activity could be nurtured at different stages of education including higher levels. The (re)discovering of interests and their channelling in early education, though, requires adequate and flexible support from parents, teachers or mentors. When studying the lives of innovators, Wagner (2015) reveals the presence of key figures who defied and still defy convention in order to cater for specific needs of their mentees. Their encouragement to innovators is an encouragement to play, explore and learn from it: *myself (educator, mentor), I am letting you do so, I am with you all the way despite challenges encountered (including institutional constraints)*.

Furthermore, and following Amabile's perspective on systemic creativity (1998), Wagner (2015) conceives of *culture* as an appropriate and

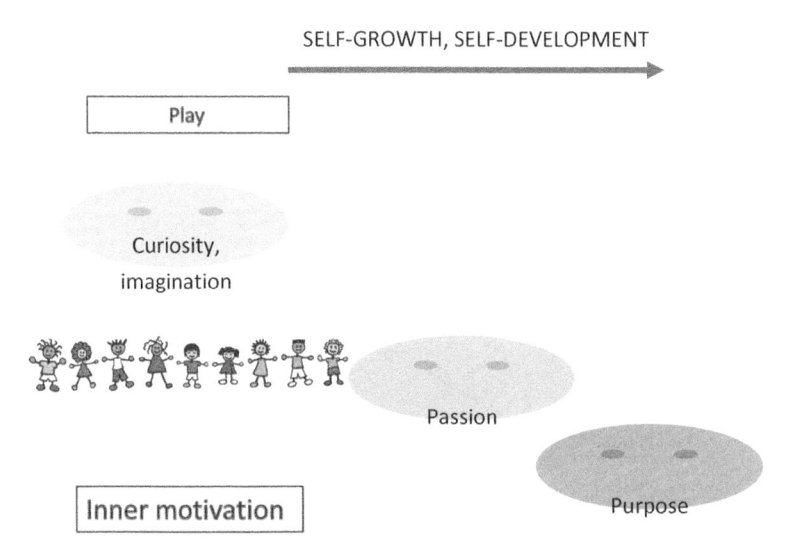

Fig. 3.2 Developing innovation in children

embracing environment of elements under which and from an early age, creators can nurture their inner motivations, passions, purposes, skills and knowledge. An appropriate innovation culture is thus designed to encourage diversity not only in catering for different types of innovators (social, commercial) or their thinking (i.e. diverging and converging) but also in the alignment of support by mentors (parents, teachers, etc).

As the Fig. 3.3 shows, according to Wagner (2015), play could also potentially contribute to develop individuals' traits/skills essential for innovation (persistence, imagination, ability to pose questions, continuous curiosity, integrative thinking, collaboration, a bias towards experimentation/action), thus shaping a notion of a creative subject as mentioned in the previous chapter of this book.

By linking play with the nurturing of innovation skills and the fuelling of a sense of purpose, by relating such nurturing to appropriate mentoring or tutoring and by acknowledging the importance of an innovation-aware culture, Wagner (2015) is effectively proposing *a system for cultivating creativity/innovation through play as a practice*. Figure 3.3 shows how, in such a system, different elements are to interact. As a system, (management) education is to provide or support the development of such

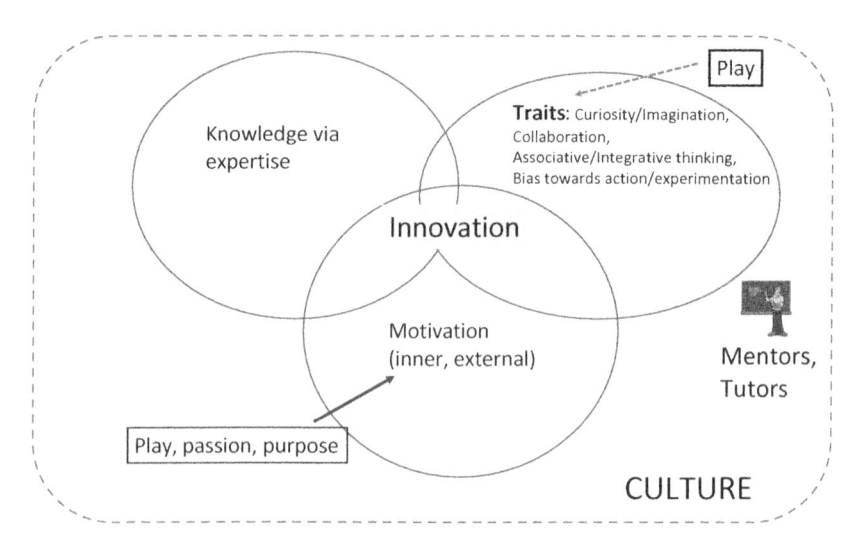

Fig. 3.3 A 'culture' system for innovation (inspired in Wagner)

elements, and under the overall objectives of governing programmes like the ones mentioned earlier.

Wagner's approach, however, leaves limited space for 'other' ways of thinking or being about innovation or creativity, including those deemed as not necessarily linked to economic growth, 'professional' or 'big' creativity (Kaufman and Beghetto 2009). More could be said about the role of play in enabling both creativity and failure to flourish, as well as in cultivating and rediscovering 'other' and less innovation-driven creativities in management education by individuals, also with a view that inner motivations or purposes might also change through time.

Inner Enthusiasm

The French pedagogist André Stern (2018) pursues the idea of play for early education even further, by arguing that we could support children to conceive of their early life as a continuous play, sometimes interrupted by having to do other things (eat, sleep). He argues that rather than focusing on developing better learning methods or approaches to support children's education, adults and teachers need to create appropriate conditions, processes and support to help children discover what they enjoy, even if that means changing interests and perspectives along the way.

All of this is because, Stern (2018) argues, children are already equipped with an inner energy to play and live without many constraints. Play is then the manifestation of such inner energy in which learning, as observed, nurtured or assessed by adults, takes place. As parents and educators, we need to let that energy flow.

Therefore, inner energy/enthusiasm could be a better word to relate to what children do in education. With enthusiasm, children marvel at what we as adults consider 'little things' and can engage with them as if they were all real, making us also wonder. Working closely, but not too close, to forms of education that focus on facilitating conditions for learning (Montessori, Vygotsky), Stern (2018) considers that children *do not* need to know much about established boundaries or conventions when learning/discovering.

Moreover, Stern (2018) argues, when children develop an interest or curiosity for something (and that does not need to be taken as long-term interest), we as parents/educators are to *engage* in the social networks and patterns of interaction that this interest involves, even if this means rearranging our 'other' commitments, including formal schooling or work. This also requires us as parents or educators *not to* promote patterns of interaction where we 'know better' than children, because we could be reinforcing the idea that learning/discovering is a game avoiding getting caught in ignorance.

Some of Stern's ideas resonate in my current life situation as a father of twins. Sometimes, I ask them questions that I know they cannot answer, where answering will make them feel guilty. With this, we enter the unhelpful dynamics of: 'I told you so!' in our interactions. Increasingly, I have become a bit more aware that this pattern could take their creativity into the path of devising answers or responses that dodge the question. My wife keeps suggesting we should then shift our children's attention to something else when we enter this type of game. I have also become more aware of my habit of being the first at imposing boundaries when children ask questions. And I am a bit more mindful of and compassionate with myself and them when I fail to please them.

To these concerns or our anxieties about failing as parents, Stern (2018) would perhaps advise us just to forget about dodgy questioning/dodgy answering patterns of interaction or communication, or change them to slightly different ones where we ask/answer more open questions and become enthusiastic partners in looking together for their answers.

Like Wagner (2015), Stern (2018) highlights the importance of inner elements and activities (play) to drive individual creativity; they are to drive the support offered by external elements (i.e. parents, schools, sports or science fiction groups). What Stern (2018) could better consider is the challenges surrounding a shift in our interactions with those external elements: our sense of or identities of selves (parents, educators, children) and of others who might not be enthusiastic at all, how to understand or manage these (Craft 2003). These are challenges that require time to address.

For a start, perhaps we could have a bit more time to reflect on or even *do nothing* with our children. That could also be considered a way of using our inner energies and spending idle time!

Living a Creative Life

> Living a [creative] life that is driven more strongly by curiosity than by fear… I always thank the process…Gratitude, always. Always, gratitude. (Gilbert 2015, pp. 9, 75, brackets added)

> You and I and everyone you know are descended from tens of thousands of years of makers…We are all makers by design…Your creativity is way older than you are, way older than any of us… and inspiration is still trying to find you. (p. 89)

> Try saying this: I enjoy my creativity…[and] stop complaining… Creativity can be heard talking: *Stay with me…come back to me…trust me.* (pp. 117–118, 147)

> There is no dishonour in having a job. What is dishonourable is scaring away your creativity by demanding that it pays for your entire existence…You may want your work to be perfect, in other words; I just want mine to be finished. (pp. 155, 177)

> Be careful with yourself…be careful about safeguarding your future but also safeguarding your sanity. (p. 107)

For the writer Elizabeth Gilbert (2015), creativity is a sort of inspirational and unpredictable **muse**, an old lady whose wealth is distributed in mysterious ways and can bless us with a charming, interesting, passionate existence (p. 42). As individuals, we are to value creativity's callings, committing our lives to work with it patiently and with a sense of awe, humility and gratefulness. If we have been called to exert our creativity, we can work silently and diligently, and in this way commune with the universe via our creative activities, keeping our sanity and that of those around us whenever possible.

Despite promoting humility and respect for how things unfold in our lives and those of others around us, in Gilbert (2015)'s view of creativity, it is not fully clear how else creativity can be pursued in 'other' ways or with alternative visions about what can be achieved by practicing something of interest to individual selves (i.e. writing). In a contradictory way, Gilbert (2015) seems to almost dismiss those who 'fail' in adopting her suggestions for creativity, and potentially dilutes this claim in arguing that like herself, we can (or should) commit our entire lives to creativity and just take failures in our stride: not doing so would mean we are not 'cut out' to achieve what we want to achieve. A bit more on enabling individual creators to be more (self) compassionate as a way of building self-acceptance, and (re)discovering 'other' possibilities for our creativity in the light of failures, could be of great value to complement what Gilbert (2015) is proposing.

LEARNING TO LEARN

A (former) polar explorer, translator and engineer, Engineering Professor Barbara Oakley (2014) proposes a way of learning to help those who are not very good friends of learning numbers, math or 'hard science'. Her approach is based on an understanding of how the human brain works. For Oakley (2014), in our development as human beings we have been able to **combine attention with diffusion**. These two activities are reflected in the functioning of the brain when learning something new or revising something we have 'learned' before.

After periods of intense focus (i.e. learning a new idea, solving a maths problem), the brain needs to relax in order to generate connections between apparently disparate other ideas that reside in distant areas of our neural networks (Oakley 2014). Relaxation can take many forms from going for a walk/run to going to the gym, playing (video) games, talking to friends or getting into social media.

In combining attention and relaxation, Oakley (2014) is also aware of *procrastination* as a habit that can be unlearned. As human beings, and partly due to our desire to get quick rewards for what we achieve, procrastination involves cues that our brains sense and act upon. That is why as learners, we get into automatic or unconscious routines of quick reward-seeking at the potential expense of routines more beneficial for retaining what we learn, like recalling, spacing our practice or scaffolding.

As Fig. 3.4 shows, Oakley (2014) instils a different focus on our learning that values process as much as content and devolves the responsibility to seek meaningful rewards to learners. This, according to Oakley, can contribute to our long-life learning. Oakley (2014) also advocates the need for learners to practice what we learn—in frequent or distributed ways—to visualise and even musicalize ideas, concepts or formulas and to retain their sense of self-worth and confidence.

Learners are to practice also in response to environmental challenges that they could encounter. We are to persevere, believe in ourselves and have a vision of who we want to become as a result of our learning. Only the acquisition of some basic knowledge can lead students to realise possibilities to expand on it and contribute with new knowledge. Like Gilbert (2015), Oakley argues that 'lady luck favours those who practice'. Meaningful practice needs to happen even in the face of low motivation or discouragement. To achieve meaning, it is important to sparse or distribute it, combining it with diffusion as mentioned earlier.

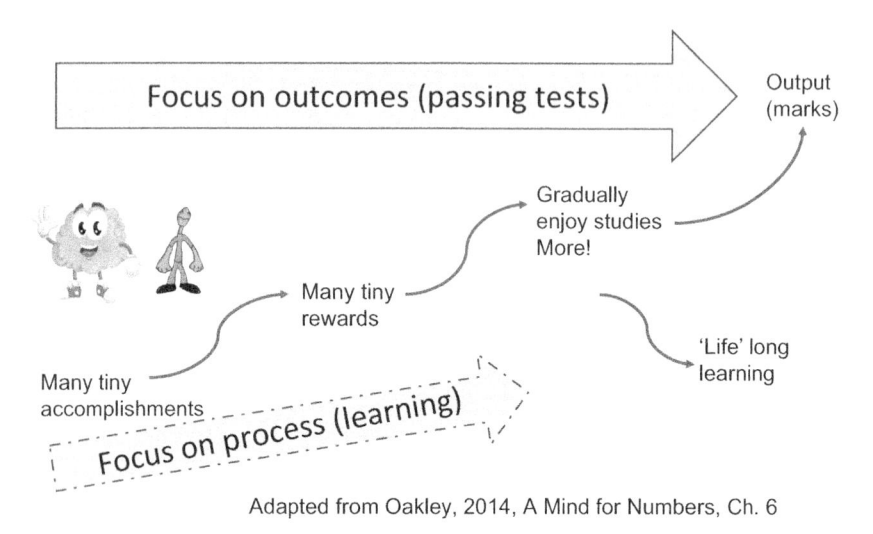

Adapted from Oakley, 2014, A Mind for Numbers, Ch. 6

Fig. 3.4 Learning how to learn

As a similar critique to Gilbert (2015)'s ideas, it could well be that rather than reinforcing the importance of success in learning (Oakley 2014), failing or failure could help students to reflect, take stock and (re)define 'other' ways of gaining or sustaining their self-confidence in the light of soft tyrannies, if not thinking about who we really want to become as purposefully driven individuals.

Learning by Interconnecting

For the authors Mary Catherine Bateson (1994) and Alfonso Montuori (2012), learning is a series of processes which we as human beings undertake in our continuous adapting to the flows of events in our lives. This adapting is driven by our innate capability to *differentiate* what works and does not, according to circumstances. From a biological/ecological stance, Bateson (1994) conceives of this difference as arising in communication, a general phenomenon that can make us connect with other living and non-living entities.

This ability to notice and act on difference, Bateson (1994) argues, is lost in education. Children's education is 'compartmentalised'; they must leave their own selves, their notions of participation in different conversations, rituals and games, behind. Educational systems promise to shape a new and independent self which, stripped of the ability of learning as interconnecting, could end up conforming to norms, fearful of change and without a repertoire of abilities to converse and co-interact with others and the natural environment (Montuori 2012). Such selves could lose their awareness about them being part of a larger 'whole' (planet, universe), and thus to dismiss any concern that has to do with it. Mary Catherine Bateson (1994) says:

> The best learners are children, not children segregated in schools but children at play, zestfully busy exploring their own homes, families, neighbourhoods, languages, conjuring up possible and impossible worlds of imagination. Only a little way from the front door, in other parts of the city or in forest or meadow, exploration continues to be possible throughout life. (M.C. Bateson 1994, p. 73)

For both Bateson (1994) and Montuori (2012), learning happens everywhere; it becomes continuous inventing, improvising, trying and reflecting/ realising. Learning is about openness and collaboration, where selves are considered contingent to the situations and contexts where they are interacting with others, as they continuously (re) create themselves and the world around them (Montuori 2012). With this degree of openness, individuals could become more accepting of how we relate to the world around us, and how our different interpretations about it could help us to co-improvise in our dealings with situations.

With the above, these authors speak about the importance of instilling continuous self-awareness of interactions between themselves and others (human and non-human). Both children and adults would need to nurture a sort of peripheral vision in which their attention (derived from also having diverse mental models and metaphors) can switch accordingly as they unfold through life. This vision would aim to enable engagement with instead of reproduction of the world around us (Montuori 2012).

Although Bateson and Montuori do not directly dismiss the importance of schools in nurturing this type of learning, they suggest that it is important to equip children and adults to be able to improvise and 'compose' their lives as they see fit. Developing appropriate and diverse systems metaphors of life and death could be a key element of education, in which people learn to care for themselves as they learn to care for others.

With this systemic idea of learning, individual or collective selves could become part of larger wholes, and the bigger the whole becomes in conversations/interactions, the better for all of us. From this self-awareness, what could emerge is that our notion of 'self' is a mutable, dynamic, fluid one, which relates to others' according to ideas, rituals, norms or metaphors considered or not useful for certain contexts and situations. Self becomes a self that continuously learns to differentiate and connect these and other elements. This idea will be explored further in the book.

Still though, Bateson (1994) acknowledges that some situations (i.e. being the dean of an academic faculty) require the adoption of a role for a self to the potential detriment of other roles (i.e. playful mother). And Montuori (2012) advocates that all selves can abandon previously acquired learnings in order to connect and synthesise new one(s). Beyond promoting interconnected communications in learning, more needs to be said about fostering or sustaining (radical) interactions or rethinking about ourselves in the light of power relations, and their emerging tensions and contradictions for our ideas about ourselves as creative as well as (self) compassionate individuals (Córdoba-Pachón 2019). To address this, a possibility could be looking at other ways than social communication to gain awareness of the interactions that contribute to shaping our ideas about us and others.

CREATIVE SCHOOLS

Adopting a level of analysis of early education and using systems ideas, Ken Robinson and Lou Aronica (2016) claim that early (school-level education) is also currently, and worldwide, at a crossroads. A standardisation global movement has advanced to the point that early education worldwide could be conceived of now as a machine: children are separated by age; they are taught different subjects during a day; there is little time for play; and tests, as well as relevant subjects (science, technology, engineering, mathematics), take precedence over other subjects or forms of assessment. This is in order to 'help' students secure specific types of employment that will contribute to increased economic growth in their countries.

To the above situation and somehow similar to the previously presented perspective on interconnected learning, Robinson and Aronica (2016) advocate an organic, complex adaptive systems view of education to nurture creativity. This means that education is to be focused on addressing each child's specific needs whilst enabling flexibility and responsiveness to respond to emerging societal demands (i.e. economic growth, sustainability). With their examples, these authors advocate practices like tailoring assessments for when students feel ready to be assessed or promoting continuous and individualised practicing. This is to be done by considering that children have often succumbed to traditional systems, so a change in their mindset as well as the mindset of educators is needed.

To enact change, Robinson and Aronica (2016) advocate the importance of having appropriate theories. It is said that as human beings we find it difficult to change. Educational schooling systems are to enable a shift in what education means, involving different stakeholders in redefining their purposes. New meanings can come from what is needed in their localities, and students can be enticed to see that formal schooling is just one possibility or option where they can come to learn what they are interested in learning. Students' learning can unfold at their own pace and be linked to practical learning that can be nurtured in 'outside' organisations.

What is not fully clear in Robinson and Aronica (2016) 's approach is how such a new focus on needs and personalised attention is to co-exist with the old one(s). A theory of change could be regarded by many in institutions as an alien threat, or if accepted, an excluding or marginalising one. Moreover, the influence of soft tyrannies needs to be factored in when promoting change, if change involves letting people *reveal* their needs, talk to each other about them, network to ensure adequate support or resources or the like: these practices could easily become governing technologies via standardisation as discussed previously. Educators would need to find ways to address such 'change' and incomplete enterprises in consideration of our purposes to stay sane, offer meaningful and diverse support to our students and manage ourselves within educational systems.

This is not to say that we would not embrace change: on the contrary and for a start, we would need to think, as has been suggested initially by Bateson (1994) and Montuori (2012) above, on how to shift our own identities or sense of ourselves, those of our students or others, and if or how we would need to align them to what is proposed. In other words, we would need to reflect on *becoming creative about being creative* in the light of soft tyrannies and do this also in our personal lives (Córdoba-Pachón 2019). A focus on interactions might be also complemented by adopting different roles or practices (i.e. play), all of this with attitudes like awareness, playfulness, seriousness or self-compassion to help ourselves and others.

Reflections

The above review of efforts to nurture creativity reveals the importance of flexibility when it comes to understanding and directing the inner energy/enthusiasm individuals all seem to have: a strong influence of our biological condition as human beings determines that we have evolved and that we can use our creativity to continue doing so. This inner flexibility/energy could positively impact future creativity. It could also be channelled through activities like play.

Furthermore, there is an inherited assumption that there is something 'out there' (daily life, universe, creativity education) which unfolds through interactions between (individual) systems and their elements, and that we use our energy, enthusiasm, awareness, resources or communication skills to connect with it and other people or things within. Connection could happen in two ways: (a) via our inner flexibility/enthusiasm (Gilbert, Stern, Bateson, Montuori, Craft, Oakley, Robinson and Aronica) or (b) via awareness of who we are or could become with others (Craft, Bateson, Robinson and Aronica) as shown in Fig. 3.5.

In Fig. 3.5, the connecting with 'other' people or things (via making the dotted arrows continuous) requires further critical thinking. Our inner selves are to be nurtured via creativity whilst becoming disconnected from each other or compartmentalised; unstructured or structured play

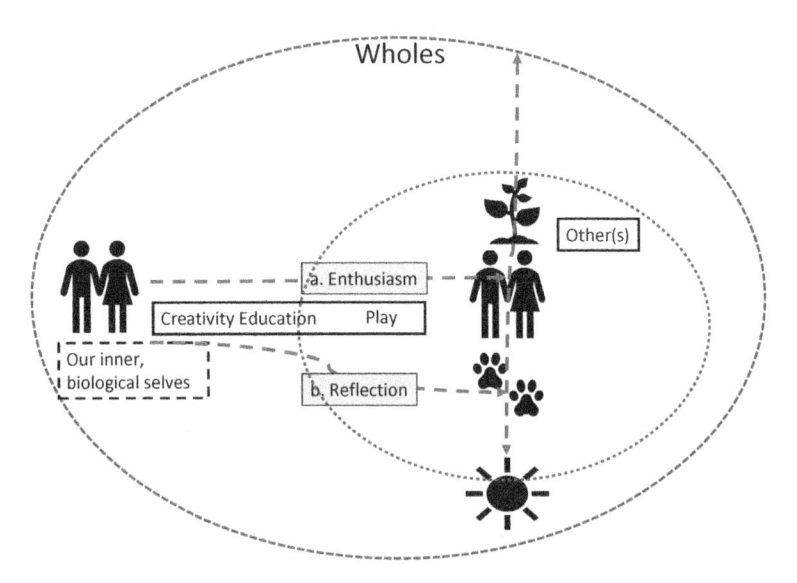

Fig. 3.5 A systemic paradox in nurturing creativity

activities are to channel passions, purposes or enthusiasm into something more societally 'meaningful' (i.e. innovation). This could be conceived of as a **systemic paradox**: an individual self is already part of a 'whole' (universe) whilst having to 'practice', 'develop' or 'grow' to gain their full membership of this and others (society, organisations), using their inner energies or resources to do so and via nurturing creativity.

In the light of the examined initiatives to nurture creativity education within soft tyrannies for management education, we would need to address this paradox and the tensions or dilemmas that it could involve for individual selves. Doing so could offer clarity on how creativity could better contribute to improve selves' education and our lives in general. It becomes important to promote inclusivity, critical reflection and self-compassion in our creativity (re)discovery efforts.

In the next chapter of this book, a further analysis and reflections on the educational potential of governmentality are conducted, and a systemic space of individual and collective roles and practices to allow selves deal with the paradox is proposed.

Conclusion

This chapter has continued a critical analysis of creativity in management education. It has done so by reviewing some of the current and valuable efforts to nurture creativity in education, highlighting how as individual selves we are to channel or use our own inner energy, enthusiasm, interests, passions or sense of purpose to become creative, and how learning environments could facilitate or inhibit it.

In reviewing different efforts for creativity, a key systemic paradox or contradiction has been identified: using our inner selves, we are to (self) develop to connect with bigger 'wholes' (i.e. universe) via creativity whilst *already* being part of them. This might not be possible unless a more systemic view of us and others as individuals is developed. To address this paradox, a further review of Foucault's governmentality is undertaken in the next chapter of this book.

References

Amabile, T. (1998, September–October). How to Kill Creativity. *Harvard Business Review, 1998*, 77–87.

Bateson, M. C. (1994). *Peripheral Visions: Learning Along the Way*. New York: Harper.

Córdoba-Pachón, J. R. (2019). *Managing Creativity: A Systems Thinking Journey*. London: Routledge.

Craft, A. (2001). Little c Creativity. In A. Craft, B. Jeffrey, & M. Leibling (Eds.), *Creativity in Education* (pp. 45–51). London: Continuum.

Craft, A. (2003). The Limits to Creativity in Education: Dilemmas for the Educator. *British Journal of Educational Studies, 51*(2), 113–127.

Csikszentmihalyi, M. (1988). Society, Culture and Person: A Systems View of Creativity. In M. Csikszentmihalyi (Ed.), *The Systems Model of Creativity: The Collected Works of Mihaly Csikszentmihalyi* (pp. 47–61). Dordrecht: Springer.

Gardner, H. (2011). *Creating Minds: An Anatomy of Creativity Seen Through the Lives of Freud, Einstein, Picasso, Stravinsky, Eliot, Graham, and Gandhi*. New York: Basic Books. Reprinted Edition.

Gilbert, E. (2015). *Big Magic: Creative Living Beyond Fear*. London: Bloomsbury.

Kaufman, J., & Beghetto, R. (2009). Beyond Big and Little: The Four C Model of Creativity. *Review of General Psychology, 13*(1), 1–12.

Montuori, A. (2012). Creative Inquiry: Confronting the Challenges of Scholarship in the 21st Century. *Futures, 44*, 64–70.

Oakley, B. (2014). *A Mind for Numbers*. New York: Tarcher/Putnam.
Robinson, K., & Aronica, L. (2016). *Creative Schools*. New York: Penguin.
Stern, A. (2018). Tous Enthousiastes! Retrouvez Votre Énergie d'Enfant. Paris: Editions Horay.
Wagner, T. (2015). *Creating Innovators: The Making of Young People Who Will Change the World*. New York: Scribner, Simon and Schuster, Inc.

CHAPTER 4

A Systemic Space for Selves

Introduction

The previous two chapters of the book have offered a sense of how, as a result of the operation of soft power tyrannies or attempts to nurture creativity, there are challenges as well as opportunities for its rediscovery. A dominant strong notion of inner energetic individual 'self' is pervading what we think creative people are to be or do. That self is to continuously develop or grow, physically, socially and mentally. A good environment is required for her to interact with others, to practice or play, and ultimately become aligned to wider societal governing programmes of economic growth and knowledge disciplining. All of this whilst already being part of a universe but having to work hard to acquire or maintain such membership. **A systemic paradox.**

In this chapter I present a type of enquiry for the governed individual self by contextualising and extending the scope of Foucault's governmentality for education. Such an enquiry could play multifarious educational roles for individuals (Liebmann-Schaub 1989; Peters and Besley 2007; Noguera 2009), and in this way help us perform and imagine diverse 'public' (collective) or 'private' (individual) roles and practices. With this possibility, a systemic space for individual selves to operate our creativities (whatever we understand by them) is proposed.

The chapter is organised as follows. I contextualise the notion of individual selves within the knowledge fields of creativity and applied systems thinking, arguing that in those there is a possibility for selves to become more 'fluid'. By extending the scope of Foucault's governmentality, it would be possible to include varied roles and practices for individual selves and address the paradox encountered for them. A systemic space for diverse selves' roles and practices to operate in the light of soft tyrannies for management education is proposed.

Traces of the Individual Self in Creativity and Applied Systems Thinking Research

The 'I' in Creativity

A brief historical review of the creativity field in the twentieth century shows how early studies of groups of talented individuals and families based on their genes were superseded by the mid-century popularisation of the idea that any individual could become creative. Large-scale production and service consumerism provided opportunities for people to exert their creative choices (Pope 2005). Individual-centred creativity research gained prominence aided by claims that creativity was different from intelligence (Guilford 1950) and by the emergence of psychological tests to support this claim (i.e. Torrance 1981).

Alternative conceptions about creative individuals suggested that it was individuals in continuous interactions with their surroundings which contributed to them exhibiting creative skills or personality traits (Barron 1968, 1972). With this a more systemic view of creativity gained relevance, one in which the individual 'I' and her inner elements acquired a degree of mobility and fluency in the face of 'other' individual, collective or environmental ones (Csikszentmihalyi 1988; Montuori and Purser 1995; Amabile 1998).

Following the work of other creativity researchers (Amabile 1998; Csikszentmihalyi 1988, 1996; Montuori and Purser 1995; Sawyer 2006; Glavenau 2010), I have previously distinguished two different traditions or lineages unfolding in the field of creativity in the twentieth- and twenty-first centuries (Córdoba-Pachón 2019): (a) one focused on creativity as residing in the individual, and (b) another that regards creativity as a systemic, socio-culturally driven, emergent phenomenon that results from the interaction between individuals and their surroundings or environments (Glavenau et al. 2019). By calling the above lineages or traditions, my aim was to relate the pursuit of a creative element (idea, product, process) to how individuals (including myself) could become part of and connected to diverse groups.

In the pursuit of a creative project and following a notion of creativity as a systemic by-product of interactions between creators and others (Córdoba-Pachón 2019), I became more consciously aware of the importance of borrowing ideas from other disciplines or knowledge settlements (i.e. organisations, partnerships) to promote creativity. However, doing so was challenging. I also acknowledged the importance of my own well-being as a creative and continuous effort, and how the 'I' also needed to be critical of existing creativity manifestations in Westernised societies. Living a creative life would also require ethical reflection on this 'I' idea to reconcile us as individuals with ourselves and our surroundings (Córdoba-Pachón 2019).

Whilst a systemic, socio-cultural tradition for creativity research and practice has gained prominence in the last few years (Clapp 2017; Glavenau et al. 2019), there is still, at least, a sort of methodological dependency on the notion of individual creators (Glavenau 2010). The individual self or 'I' keeps popping up for example as an element of systems models of creativity, or as a resource for narratives to represent how creators 'successfully made it' (Dobelli 2013; Hanson 2013). Failure is not yet fully articulated in such narratives (Hanson 2013).

Moreover, at our educational institutions, we keep reinforcing a narrow idea of individual success. We do not, for instance, invite people who failed to tell students how they did it and what they learned from failure unless they recover from it and later succeed. This is despite some attempts to 'distribute' creativity beyond individuals and infuse a sense of awareness in areas like education. Clapp (2017), for example, advocates studying the 'biography' of an idea to enthuse students to acknowledge how ideas are not the result of individuals working alone but often in collaboration with others. Although valuable in practice (more on this later in this book), this might not help individual selves deal with the paradox of belonging whilst having to gain membership of 'wholes', unless a more critical stance is taken to inform enquiry.

As Dobelli (2013) says, when it comes to 'success', the world is full of 'cemeteries' which we should visit. And cemeteries are normally organised in individual tombs of different forms and shapes. We could use this assumption to our advantage to further enquiry into 'other' roles for individual selves than those related to their creative and individual success or failure in management education. Doing this could provide key insights on how to promote creativity rediscovery for ourselves and others, making us more aware of nuances, tensions, dilemmas, activities or possibilities.

The 'System' and the Individual Selves

The field of applied systems thinking (AST) follows a sort of reverse historical unfolding to that of creativity, despite having some common origin: the study of populations. Ludwig von Bertalanffy (1968) proposed a general theory of systems to account for principles that could be used to understand the systemic nature of living beings and societies. This theory seemed to echo or be followed by a general interest in how the management of welfare could be improved after successive world wars. An issue worthy of being adequately governed.

Along a similar line of enquiry to that of von Bertalanffy, the philosopher and systems thinker Churchman (1968) acknowledged the essentiality of subjecting the assumptions and value judgments of decision-makers to debate in the planning of societal improvements. He proposed the idea of a system as an *inter-subjective construction*, whose boundaries are strongly related to the values of those defining it. With this idea, Churchman encouraged planners and decision-makers to consider the impacts of improvements in the light of their potential consequences for present and future generations. Ethics of 'heroism' (Churchman 1968, referred to the individual hero planner) invited people to acknowledge the limitations of their individual thinking and enter dialogue or debate with others to improve managerial decisions and their resulting consequences.

Following Churchman and in the UK and Europe, social theory and philosophy have informed the development of methodological approaches that seek systemic social improvements (Ulrich 1983; Midgley 2000; Jackson 2003; Córdoba-Pachón and Midgley 2006). However, any focus on the individual self seems to be subsumed into the definition and debate of systems boundaries in debate.

This is more evident in the approach of Banathy (1973), in which educational systems could be designed to play a twofold role: to contribute to serve societal needs whilst challenging them to make education more inclusive and participative. Although there is a focus on needs and individual internalisation of systems ideas, it is the individual who must make sense of both herself and the systems by changing her worldviews or helping others do so. The systemic paradox previously identified in this book (an individual self having to develop to connect to wholes whilst already being part of them) could be further reinforced with no further guidance for systemically minded individuals on how to deal with it.

Therefore, a focus on systems design could leave other specific individual needs out of the enquiry. The Churchman-inspired hero systems planners could potentially limit themselves to their roles of 'agents' or 'facilitators' within collectively driven processes of knowledge generation. Their own ethics could become related to locally defined social improvements (Midgley 2000), needing further expertise and interest as facilitators to bring other issues of concern to the debate.

And depending on how 'rich' or 'inclusive' systems methodologies or those facilitating interventions with them are, their 'other' and individual experiences might (not) be fully included in systemic enquiry (Córdoba-Pachón 2011). Applied systems methodologies could be a source of individual awareness and creativity, as they have been to myself and many others in recent years. But we still would need to be more inclusive of other issues or human experiences from ourselves or others in enquiry, and how other forms of practice than systems methodologies could also be brought into it.

Other systems thinkers like Maturana and Varela (1998), Varela, Shear and Thompson (1993), or Wright (2017) have considered the individual self as an instrument for scientific enquiry. Maturana and Varela (1998) argue that because of our biological nature as living beings, our cognitive processes are self-producing, in other words, determined by the history of our interactions (in language conversation) with others. To this limitation and in similar ways to Bateson (1994) as presented earlier in this book, we could learn a bit more by declaring our ignorance to situations and entering respectful dialogue or conversations with others.

In this way, the individual self could become a less fixed and a more **fluid one** whose role is that of inviting herself to co-create with other selves. Varela, Thompson and Shear (1993) bring forth Buddhist thinking to reinforce the view that in Western scientific enquiry, the individual self is never to be fully found or represented. Trying to account for her via fixed, 'objective' or measurable images or narratives will limit the interactions of those observing as well as those being observed and will miss relevant 'data'.

In a similar yet potentially less radical way to Bateson (1994) and Montuori (2012), what these authors suggest is that the individual self could be better conceived of as a point of encounter and reflection. Those researching her could be encouraged to abandon our 'street fighter' mentality in science and replace it by a more collaborative, compassionate, planetary, ecologically and universally driven one from which our enquiries could become richer and more relevant to our societies.

An evolutionary psychologist, Wright (2017) also draws on Buddhism to challenge the idea of a fixed, homogenous self that makes all decisions and is in full control. Without fully advocating that the 'self' does not exist, Wright (2017) puts forward the idea of an individual self as a space of competition between different neural networks. The operation of such networks is heavily influenced by an inherited biological drive to pass on genes to the next generation, and cognitive rewards like anticipated pleasure or a sense of immanence. According to Wright (2017), Buddhist thinking can invite individual selves to observe themselves and distance from, manage or disown ideas or feelings that we consider essential for our existence.

Figure 4.1 shows that in creativity and systems thinking there is a 'pull down' to fix or leave out considerations about individual selves, a pull that is reinforced by the assumption that individual selves need to be or become 'normal' ones (i.e. without serious mental health problems) in enquiry. Despite the support offered in designing educational systems via systems methodologies and ideas, to achieve improvements creative individual selves need to be able to individually identify and manage contradictions in their own lives (Csikszentmihalyi 1996) or get appropriate help (a 'shrink') to do so (Barron 1997).

Fig. 4.1 Selves, wholes and soft tyrannies

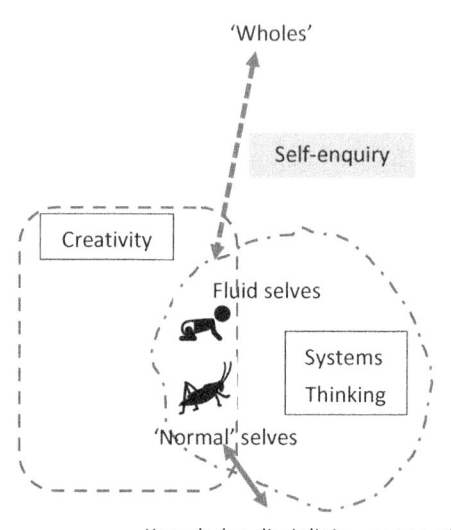

Nevertheless, there are some ideas within these fields that seem to regard the individual self as fluid or diverse. This is uplifting and could help us as educators and others involved or affected by management education further explore other nurturing ways to help ourselves and other people deal with the systemic paradox mentioned above via creativity.

Within soft tyrannies, there could be different directions to 'go' for free individual selves, including that of striving to let go of themselves, or at least some of the ideas we think are essential for ourselves. To frame these and to address the previously identified paradox for us, a further interpretation of the scope of Foucault's governmentality is offered in the next sections of this chapter.

Revisiting Governmentality

From studies that challenge neoliberal thinking in policymaking or organisational management and modern life (Dean 2009) to critiques of the impacts of information and communication technologies in organisations and government (Zuboff 1989; Willcocks 2006; Henman 2014) or education (Drummond 2003; McClam and Flores-Scott 2012), one can see a diversity of interpretations and uses of Foucault's notion of governmentality.

What appears to be a contentious issue in several of these is how far the critiques could end up simply rehearsing or adopting Foucault's own claims about governmentality as a multifarious and often limiting or constraining notion. A richer understanding of what Foucault was aiming at with his work could help enquiry into creativity education go beyond focusing on issues of disciplining, surveillance or resistance (us and them or vice-versa), and open possibilities for productive, ethically driven counter-conduct of individual selves as creative subjects (Kendall and Wickham 1999; Willcocks 2006; Córdoba-Pachón 2006, 2019).

To meet this aim, it needs to be said that Foucault (1984) advocates a possibility of having different, fluid, less fixated selves as initially proposed in this chapter. He talks about the European Enlightenment as a continuous attitude towards what constitutes our present time (p. 37):

> Enlightenment, as we see, must not be conceived of as a general process affecting all humanity; it must not be conceived of as an obligation [dare to know!] prescribed to individuals; it now appears as a political problem. The question, in any event, is that of knowing how the use of reason can take the

public form that it requires, how the audacity to know [personally, privately] can be exercised in broad daylight, while individuals are obeying as scrupulously as possible. (brackets added)

For Foucault (1984), the Enlightenment epoch has shown how philosophy could be a tool for rational enquiry, and a way of inspiring others in how it could be used to operate within power relations (Foucault 1984). As an enquiring tool, an enlightenment philosopher had to pay her collective duties (i.e. contribute to explain phenomena, generate knowledge, or both). She could also make use of her private, 'inner' and universally available 'reasoning' so that she could try or explore 'other' ways of governing herself, her thinking and acting (Foucault 1984).

Moreover, Foucault (1984) says that as individuals we could strive to tease out what makes the present so 'unique' whilst still being perceived as recurrently emerging. This suggests that we could experiment with, **imagine**, say yes or no to possibilities in the 'wholes' we think we are part of, in other words, that we could still be creative about the present, using our available freedom to enquire about and educate ourselves and others (Rose et al. 2006; Peters and Besley 2007). This is for Foucault 'A way of relating to contemporary reality … a way of thinking and feeling … of acting and behaving that one and the same time marks a relation of belonging and presents itself as a task. A bit, no doubt, like what the Greeks called an *ethos*' (Foucault 1984, p. 39).

In this line of thought, Drummond (2003) and Noguera (2009) conceive of governmentality as a methodological or analytical notion which could lead us to consider its potential **educational** power in the present. It could help us challenge what we think about ourselves as subjects whose conduct is being (self) regulated whilst we obey governmentalities. By teaching his historical work on ancient Greek sexuality (Foucault 1992), both Drummond (2003) and Noguera (2009) suggest that Foucault was **inviting others** to do the same: (a) to identify ethical aspects to change in ourselves (for instance habits); (b) to work on these aspects (for instance via education, studying, learning); and (c) with the purpose of becoming someone else (i.e. employable, mature, wise). In other words, to develop or assume different selves.

Furthermore, Foucault could have also embedded an additional educational proviso in his work: (d) to avoid permanent adherence to knowledge discourses or narratives like Greek Ethics (Foucault 1994) or Humanism as the discovery of a true self (Foucault 1984, 1994). As this present book has argued so far, this proviso could be interpreted as being continuously aware of potential normalisations of ourselves (educators, students, others) as 'creative-productive' subjects via discourses, or technologies like assessment and standardisation, whose operation could erode our individual and collective freedom.

Liebmann-Schaub (1989) also provides a reading of Foucault's earlier work which she claims leans towards an Oriental consideration of the 'Other', in capitals, that is, it points to a space of co-existence of individual selves with the **mystical**, that which can be experienced but cannot be fully spoken about. This space acts as a 'void', so that our experiences cannot be fully articulated or reasoned about via spoken language. And it operates as the **limits** of what we regard as scientific, rational or structured knowledge.

By showing that there can be an Oriental 'subtext' in Foucault's work, Liebmann-Schaub (1989) argues that Foucault embedded a subversive strategy for individual selves: it consists of showing us the logical contradictions and incompleteness of our discursive practices. If performed repeatedly, we could 'speak ceaselessly the self-destructive language [about ourselves] … and modulate its futility' (Liebmann-Schaub 1989, p. 60, brackets added). In line with this, Liebmann-Shaub (1989) also notices how Foucault explores other practices for care of the self like asceticism (Foucault 1988), praying or writing about oneself (Foucault 1992).

The above activities or practices could help individual selves take some distance from themselves (reflect), and potentially 'let go' of identified or perceived limitations, some of which are the by-product of authorship practices designed to make us 'disappear' in the operation of social functions (Foucault 1969). We can, however, use them *to our advantage* in the light of soft tyrannies for management education. We could, for instance, employ, like Foucault did, historical methods like knowledge archaeology or social genealogy to interrogate our constitution as subjects in the present (Foucault 1984; Kendall and Wickham 1999). This could help us as educators or students reveal and understand the blind spots that disciplinary knowledge generates in how we perceive the world (McClam and Flores-Scott 2012). Their experiencing could be conceding a form of power to individual selves, one that is less about social agonism, confrontation with others or transcending and more about helping us reflect and act on who or what we think we are as educational, creative subjects (Liebmann-Schaub 1989).

At a specific, individual or private level of educational analysis/enquiry, other practices like (self) writing, mindfulness meditation, improvising

(Goldie 2015), reflecting or speaking could be performed in a humorous and playful manner to help us 'strive from detachment of that [ego] reality ... [,] destroy the madness of normality and to regain true reality' (Liebmann-Schaub 1989, p. 308, brackets added). We could also reflect without focusing on its potential to help us become more aware of who we are as individuals (Wright 2017; Córdoba-Pachón 2019). It could be through iteration of these practices that we could realise limitations that we have been imposing, or that have been imposed upon us, and what we could do about them.

These and other practices though could be difficult to embrace or sustain; routine or repetitious challenges seem to be exacerbated by our individual, private roles in societies. Authoring, for example, could make us 'disappear' in the wake of wider social functions (Foucault 1969). And, we could be somehow misunderstood in our efforts to nurture creativity when educating. Foucault himself seems to have been dismissed by some of his Western contemporaries as disconcerting or inconsistent (Liebmann-Schaub 1989).

But who are we to judge how serious we or the others are? Here a more mystical perspective could provide some reassurance:

> I am going to write a book some day and the title will be I'M AN ASS, YOU ARE AN ASS. That is the most liberating thing in the world when you openly admit you are an ass. It is wonderful. When people tell me 'You are wrong'. I say: 'What can you expect from an ass?'. (Anthony de Mello, S.J. 1997, *Awareness*, p. 40)

It might be thus possible to undertake an educational enquiry into creativity within governmentality and its operational soft tyrannies for management education. By exploring Foucault's work on Greek ethics, Drummond (2003) also argues that Foucault was considering 'other people' as part of an Enlightened attitude towards the present which could be exerted in education. The intertwining of the individual and the collective that Foucault proposes for the ethos about the present involves for Drummond (2003) three key elements in what the latter terms 'educare'. These elements are (i) concern for self; (ii) concern for knowledge and (iii) concern for educands.

As educators or creative subjects, being aware of the above elements could help us to make sense of what we do or could be doing when nurturing creativity in management education. With them, we are to avoid falling into excessive collectivism or individualism when nurturing creativity in education; we could also become more aware of how as educational selves we act as (self) conduits of knowledge. Being governed as creative subjects could be an opportunity for counter-conduct by ethically governing ourselves and others in counter-conduct according to what we think needs to be thought of or done in our present.

And as the superheroes say: 'With greater power comes greater responsibility'. All of this could be developed whilst maintaining a sense of humour in who we are or what we do as creative subjects.

Towards a Systemic Space for Individual, Creative Selves

An argument can now be put forward to address the systemic paradox for individual selves noticed so far when nurturing creativity in (management) education. This paradox involved an individual self who, on the one hand, works hard to be part of a collectively oriented whole or set of wholes, whilst also already feeling or being part of them on the other.

With governmentality reinterpreted as an ethical attitude towards our present, individual selves aiming to educate themselves or others about our present situation **could do both** of the above by (1) 'working hard' to be or become socially accepted selves by teaching, learning, writing, meditating or simply being creative in education, and in this way revealing ourselves as governable subjects (Foucault 1988). And (2) letting go of these or other practices, becoming individual selves who strive to 'care' for ourselves in what we consider more meaningful or ethically relevant ways, and in doing so helping in the care of others.

The portrayed space proposed in Fig. 4.2 accounts for the potential avoidance of full extremes (collective, individual) and the inclusion of individual or collective roles as well as practices (learning, writing, speaking, meditating, humouring). The non-linear combination of roles and practices could be guided by a care ethics of self-knowledge-others as discussed above. With this space as a 'shield', it might be possible to engage with soft tyrannies in management education. In our present time (s), we are to be inevitably subjected to the operation of governing programmes (i.e. economic growth, knowledge disciplining), governing technologies (i.e. assessment, standardisation, morality) or governing functions (i.e. creativity, lack of time), whilst we can rediscover or develop our own creativities and ways of being or thinking in our present time (s) and situations of creativity education in management.

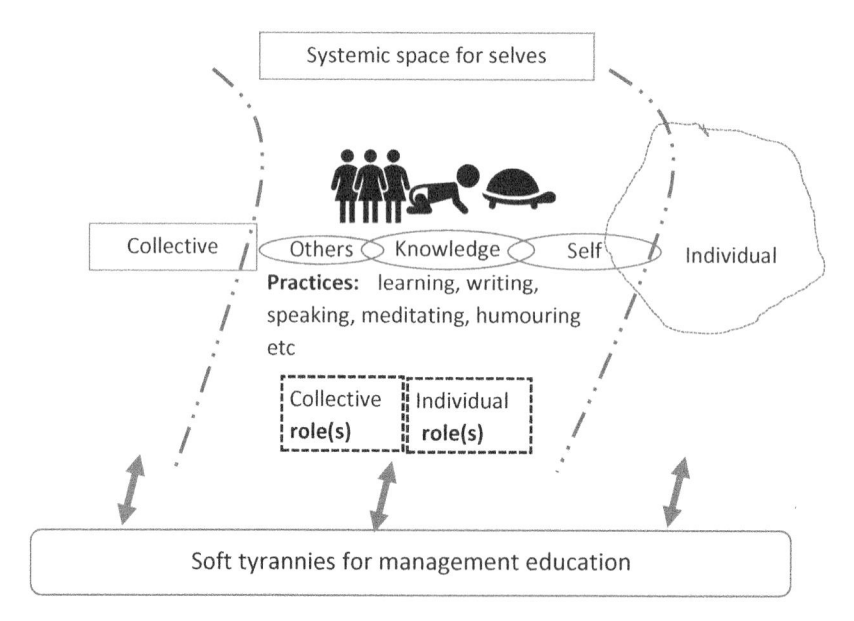

Fig. 4.2 A systemic space for selves

Concluding Remarks

This chapter has laid out the features of a space for individual selves to conceive of governmentality enquiries as educational. Following Foucault, this space involves us assuming a diversity of individual and collective roles and practices to help us all live in the present of soft tyrannies in management education whilst imagining it in other ways. The space proposed could act as an intermediary or bridge between efforts to nurture creativity via socio-cultural or systemic processes of knowledge generation. To develop this space, (self, knowledge, others) care needs to be taken to avoid extremes when assuming these to potentially erode our individual or collective freedom.

Some practices like (self) writing, speaking, learning, humouring, meditating or letting go have been elicited as possibilities to help individual selves inhabit the space proposed when adopting roles required or imagined. To inhabit the proposed space and infuse a sort of 'inner energy' to help us continue dealing with the paradox of membership identified earlier, a spirit of play is defined in the next chapter of this book.

References

Amabile, T. (1998, September–October). How to Kill Creativity. *Harvard Business Review, 76*, 77–87.
Banathy, B. (1973). *Developing a Systems View of Education – The Systems Model Approach.* Belmont: Lear Siegler, Inc./Fearon Publishers.
Barron, F. (1968). *Creativity and Personal Freedom.* London: D. Van Nostrand Company Inc..
Barron, F. (1972). Towards an Ecology of Consciousness. *Inquiry, 15*(1–4), 95–113.
Barron, F. (1997). Introduction. In F. Barron, A. Montuori, & A. Barron (Eds.), *Creators on Creating* (pp. 1–21). New York: Jeremy P. Tarcher/Penguin.
Bateson, M. C. (1994). *Peripheral Visions: Learning Along the Way.* New York: Harper.
Clapp, E. (2017). *Participatory Creativity: Introducing Access to Equity to the Creative Classroom.* New York: Routledge.
Churchman, C. W. (1968). *The Systems Approach.* New York: Dell Publishing.
Córdoba-Pachón, J. R. (2011). Embracing Human Experience in Applied Systems-Thinking. *Systems Research and Behavioral Science, 28*(6), 680–688.
Córdoba-Pachón, J. R. (2019). *Managing Creativity: A Systems Thinking Journey.* London: Routledge.
Córdoba-Pachón, J. R., & Midgley, G. (2006). Broadening the boundaries: an application of critical systems thinking to IS planning in Colombia. *Journal of the Operational Research Society, 57*(9), 1064–1080.
Csikszentmihalyi, M. (1988). Society, Culture and Person: A Systems View of Creativity. In M. Csikszentmihalyi (Ed.), *The Systems Model of Creativity: The Collected Works of Mihaly Csikszentmihalyi* (pp. 47–61). Dordrecht: Springer.
Csikszentmihalyi, M. (1996). *Creativity: Flow and the Psychology of Discovery and Invention.* New York: Harper Collins.
Dean, M. (2009). *Governmentality: Power and Rule in Modern Society.* London: Sage Publications Ltd, Second Edition.
De Mello, A. (1997). *Awareness.* Grand Rapids, Michigan (US): Zondervan.
Dobelli, R. (2013). *The Art of Thinking Clearly.* London: Sceptre.
Drummond, J. (2003). Care of the Self in a Knowledge Economy: Higher Education, Vocation and the Ethics of Michel Foucault. *Educational Philosophy and Theory, 35*(1), 57–69.
Foucault, M. (1969). What is an author? In P. Rabinow (Ed.), *The Foucault Reader: An Introduction to Foucault's Thought* (pp. 101–120). London: Penguin.
Foucault, M. (1984). What is enlightenment? In P. Rabinow (Ed.), *The Foucault Reader: An Introduction to Foucault's Thought* (pp. 32–50). London: Penguin.
Foucault, M. (1988). Tecnologías del yo (Technologies of the Self). In M. Morey (Ed.), *Tecnologías del Yo y Otros Textos Afines* (pp. 45–94). Barcelona: Ediciones Paidós.

Foucault, M. (1992). *The Use of Pleasure: The History of Sexuality Volume 2* (Translated from French by Robert Hurley). London: Penguin.

Foucault, M. (1994). The ethics of the concern for self as a practice of freedom. In P. Rabinow (Ed.), *Michel Foucault: Ethics, Subjectivity and Truth* (pp. 281–302). London: Penguin.

Glavenau, V. (2010). Principles for a Cultural Psychology of Creativity. *Culture & Psychology, 16*(2), 147–163. https://doi.org/10.1177/1354067X10361394.

Glavenau, V., Hanson, M. H., Baer, J., Clapp, E., et al. (2019). Advancing Creativity Theory and Research: A Socio-Cultural Manifesto. *The Journal of Creative Behaviour, 0*(0), 1–5. https://doi.org/10.1002/jobc.395.

Goldie, A. (2015). *The Improv Book: Improvisation for Theatre, Comedy, Education and Life*. London: Oberon Books.

Guilford, J. P. (1950). Creativity. *American Psychologist, 5*(9), 444–454.

Hanson, M. H. (2013). Author, Self, Monster: Using Foucault to Examine Functions of Creativity. *Journal of Theoretical and Psychological Psychology, 33*(1), 18–31.

Henman, P. (2014). *Governing Electronically: E-government and the Reconfiguration of Public Administration, Policy and Power* (2nd ed.). Basingstoke: Palgrave Macmillan.

Jackson, M. (2003). *Creative Holism: Systems Thinking for Managers*. Chichester: John Wiley and Sons.

Kendall, G., & Wickham, G. (1999). *Using Foucault's Methods*. London: Sage Publications Ltd..

Liebmann-Schaub, U. (1989). Foucault's oriental subtext. *PMLA (The Journal of the Modern Language Association of America), 104*(3), 306–316.

Maturana, H., & Varela, F. (1998). *The Three of Knowledge-The Biological Roots of Human Understanding*. Boston: Shambhala.

McClam, S., & Flores-Scott, E. (2012). Transdisciplinary Teaching and Research: What Is Possible in Higher Education? *Teaching in Higher Education, 17*(3), 231–243.

Midgley, G. (2000). *Systemic Intervention: Philosophy, Methodology and Practice*. New York: Kluwer Academic/Plenum Publishers.

Montuori, A. (2012). Creative Inquiry: Confronting the Challenges of Scholarship in the 21st Century. *Futures, 44,* 64–70.

Montuori, A., & Purser, R. (1995). Deconstructing the Lone Genius Myth: Toward a Contextual View of Creativity. *Journal of Humanistic Psychology, 35*(3), 69–112.

Noguera, C. (2009). La Gubernamentalidad en Los Cursos del Profesor Foucault. *Educação & Realidade, 34*(2), 21–33.

Peters, M., & Besley, A.C. (Tina). (2007). Introduction: Why Foucault? New Directions in Educational Research. In M. Peters & A. C. (Tina) Besley (Eds.), *Why Foucault? New Directors in Educational Research* (pp. 1–14). New York: Peter Lang.

Pope, R. (2005). *Creativity: Theory, History and Practice.* London: Routledge.
Rose, N., O'Malley, P., & Valverde, M. (2006). Governmentality. *Annual Review of Law and Social Sciences, 2,* 83–104.
Sawyer, K. (2006). *Explaining Creativity: The Science of Human Innovation.* New York: Oxford University Press.
Torrance, P. (1981). Empirical Validation of Criterion Referenced Indicators of Creative Ability Through a Longitudinal Study. *Creative Child and Adult Quarterly, 6,* 136–140.
Ulrich, W. (1983). *Critical Heuristics of Social Planning: A New Approach to Practical Philosophy.* Bern (Switzerland): Haupt.
Varela, F., Thompson, E., & Rosch, E. (1993). *The Embodied Mind: Cognitive Science and Human Experience.* Cambridge: MIT Press.
von Bertalanffy, L. (1968). *General Systems Theory: Foundations, Development, Applications.* New York: George Braziller.
Willcocks, L. (2006). Michel Foucault in the Social Study of ICTs – Critique and Reappraisal. *Social Science Computer Review, 24*(3), 274–295.
Wright, R. (2017). *Why Buddhism Is True – The Science and Philosophy of Meditation and Enlightenment.* New York: Simon and Schuster.
Zuboff, S. (1989). *In The Age Of The Smart Machine: The Future of Work and Power.* New York: Basic Books.

CHAPTER 5

A Spirit of Play (and Seriousness)

Introduction

The previous chapter of this book has proposed a space of multiple roles (individual, collective) and practices to ethically govern ourselves and others in the light of soft tyrannies for management education.

Like a house, this space needs to be *inhabited with some sort of spirit*. As if in the house we are to occupy we are to ensure that we do not crash against the walls or other people inhabiting it. Among other things, we could humour our learning, read, write or meditate whenever possible.

This chapter provides a way to enthuse practices with what is to be called **a spirit of play (and seriousness)**. Westernised thinking has tended to link play with personal development through socialisation. The operation of soft tyrannies has contributed to limit our ideas about play by making us think that 'there is not enough time' to do so, or that play is related to competition.

A result is that play as an activity could end up serving instrumental purposes—one of them innovation (Wagner 2015). A quick glance at the use of simulation software tools or electronic-online games for management education could provide further evidence to this claim.

As an alternative and inspired by the work of the French philosopher Jean-Paul Droit (2018), play (and seriousness) could be conceived as a kind of 'spirit', a reflective lens to help us enter, inhabit or leave the space of multiple roles and practices for individual selves in creativity. Through becoming infused with this spirit, we could let go of our ideas about

© The Author(s) 2020
J.-R. Córdoba-Pachón, *Creativity in Management Education*,
https://doi.org/10.1007/978-3-030-50960-6_5

ourselves or others through timeless and cyclical refreshing or iterating of games we can play, even if we do not fully grasp what they are about (Droit 2018). We could identify, reflect on or rewrite game rules, or abandon games altogether.

The chapter is structured as follows. A brief overview of how play is conceived nowadays is made, and how this conception bears a relation to the lack of solitary reflection for individual selves in our Westernised societies. Then play is re-contextualised outside of its normal learning role(s) and within what Droit calls the spirit of childhood (2018); a spirit of play could inherit several of the features of the spirit of childhood. A new paradox of playfulness/seriousness is defined and some methodological implications for educational enquiries about creativity in management education are drawn.

Play, Seriously?

Before entering the classroom to teach my final year management students, a question that often lingers in my mind is if and how they have nurtured their curiosity, imagination, spark or improvisation.

On the one hand, they could have been helped by opportunities to engage with experiential, artistic or sportive assessments within or outside university. There could be some students with 'natural' abilities that help them survive standardised schooling even at university. On the other, their anxiety not to fail could have made a dent in how they now see the world, driving them to follow scripts/recipes to achieve higher marks, and forget about almost everything else.

Sophia, a good friend of mine who supports students' development of academic skills at university, has noticed an increase in the degree of anxiety of our management students. The lack of time to 'play' that my seven-year-old daughter Sofia complains about seems to also affect older generations.

Moreover, many of our students decide to 'socialise in a "serious" and compartmentalised way', within physical and symbolic spaces that we created (classrooms, societies, cafes), so that they abide by constraints of physical attendance, learning progression and compliance with regulations. Anyone 'deviating' from this compartmentalisation or not being able to stand the demands of large classes, presentations or group work because of their introvert personality could find themselves 'socially' isolated or in 'trouble' (Cain 2013), even when it comes to look for jobs: another possible effect of soft tyrannies in management education.

It is time to leave a bit of the 'seriousness' that we all seem to assume in management education. I am encouraging myself to somehow and humorously fight the influence of soft tyrannies whilst obeying what they induce and conduce in all of us. As a management educator and father of small children, I acknowledge that there are some 'giant' soft tyrannies that I cannot fully defeat (Córdoba-Pachón 2019). But maybe and like Don Quixote, after writing this book, I will become more 'lucid'/'mad'/'creative' about them.

Reclaiming Reflection Within Play

In her essay 'On Reflection', Ellen Rose (2013) argues that the advent and pervasiveness of information and communication technologies (ICTs) in modern life has, among other events, contributed to a generalised sense of loss when it comes to reflection. Our Westernised societies and educational systems seem to have devalued solitary or individual reflection. Rather, and reinforced by the emerging perception about us lacking time for anything—including being creative in alternative ways to those currently being nurtured in education—what prevails is a sort of instrumentally driven, reflection-on-action type.

Rose (2013) traces some of the origins of the above situation to human reading and writing, and with it, the emergence of a sense of self: a sense that from the early twentieth century has associated ourselves with scientific, organised thinking and thus has subordinated us to it. However, Rose (2013) also rescues the importance of reading/writing in solitude. This practice can thus be linked to solitary contemplation, offering us possibilities to ponder bringing together separate ideas, imagining or wondering; in other words, to also be individually **creative**.

For Rose (2013), reclaiming solitary reflection is essential to help us as human beings restore a balance in our interactions with ourselves and others. ICTs can help us mediate or enhance such interactions. Complementing what Craft (2013) proposes to help individuals enhance their collective exploration of possibilities via exploration of 'what if' possibilities in virtual worlds, Rose (2013) reminds us that individual practicing (i.e. by reading/writing or reflecting) **could also** have societal impacts. ICTs (internet, social media, virtual learning environments) could enhance the scope of such impacts but **will not** fully replace the educational processes generating or supporting them. In this regard, individual selves could gain awareness of how ICTs get embedded into power relations, and what we could do about our own ethics in the light of technologies-reinforced power challenges and opportunities (Córdoba-Pachón 2007, 2010, 2019).

In one of the attempts to nurture creativity in early education previously reviewed in this book, it was said earlier that 'unstructured play' could help children become interested, passionate and purposeful about an aspect of their lives (Wagner 2015). Play was also deemed as an activity to help children connect the different 'worlds' that they take part in by noticing and acting on differences of communication (Bateson 1994). This was proposed to enable children and adults to adapt to emerging circumstances and challenges in their interactions with others. Many of our conversations, communications or interactions need now to respond to concerns about the natural environment and the planet (Bateson 1994).

Like ICTs and reflection-on-action (Rose 2013), a socially oriented aspect of play is also considered within several theories of early learning which have also been adopted to put forward the idea of creativity as a socio-cultural phenomenon (Glavenau 2010). Learning theorists like Vygotsky (1979) have claimed that it is only through socialisation that children are able to learn. Socialisation brings continuous and cognitive comparing and noticing of differences between children, which triggers their 'inner' capabilities to adapt by imitating what others do if not articulating their thoughts via spoken language or writing. A role for educators could be to critically embed **learning and socialisation** processes within educational ICTs design and use (Barros-Castro, Córdoba-Pachón and Pinzón-Salcedo 2014).

Under these perspectives, play as an activity becomes part of intended socialisation/learning. As a vehicle also to help convey behavioural norms and rules, solitary reflection or creativity could be confined to the periphery of more 'serious', action-based activities like instruction or assessment. The French pedagogist André Stern (2018) has also warned us about adopting this subsidiary role for play in early education. With compartmentalised, structured or unstructured play, children become confused about distinguishing between what is serious and what is not. At an early age and even later, the influence of this distinction could lead children to learn another type of play in for what we conceive of as serious games: to not get caught in doing the wrong things, including not answering what the teacher wants to hear or see (Bateson 1994; Stern 2018).

Our lives and those of others could become a game of not getting caught. In such a game and following Rose (2013) as well as Cain (2013), it can be said that silent, solitary-reflective individual selves could also be excluded or marginalised. Classrooms could become prisons for speedy learning, in which vocal, extroverted or quick-thinking personalities, the ones that educators are prone to notice, dominate. And this could also be detrimental to our creativity in education. As the academics Berg and Seeber (2016) claim:

> We need, then, to protect a time and a place for timeless [slow time, doing less, unstructured time, pausing, breathing, laughing, narrating, offline, do nothing] time, and to remind ourselves continually that this is not self-indulgent but rather crucial to intellectual work. If we don't find timeless time, there is evidence that not only our work but also our brains will suffer. (p. 28, brackets added)

What follows is an alternative idea about play which could help us counteract such dominance and foster various ways of being both reflective and creative within the space of roles and practices proposed in the previous chapter of this book.

THE SPIRIT OF CHILDHOOD

The French philosopher Jean-Paul Droit (2018) makes us aware that childhood, the term and the biological stage in our lives, has been used throughout history for a *variety* of purposes, including that of 'zeroing' children when it comes to what we call human (cognitive, moral) development, something that a fellow Frenchman Stern (Stern, 2018) has also noticed, as discussed previously in this book.

The diversity of uses of the term 'childhood' gives us opportunities to use them to our own and creative purposes. Droit (2018) proposes to rescue what he calls the 'spirit of childhood' as something that does not depend on human development or existing connotations of the term. About this he says:

> I call the spirit of childhood a way to be in the world that does not have anything to do with age or competences. A look that gets surprised, that does not know how to talk about what it sees, or that does not speak about it in a wise or clever way ... [a way of being] without the possibility to take some distance from emotions ... ignoring commitments, the means, the protocols [the rules] ... [It is pure] desire, and nothing else. (Droit 2018, p. 24, brackets added, my own translation from Spanish edition)

For Droit (2018), this spirit of childhood could also be critical of the natural view of children that often influences us nowadays, and which could also be reinforcing the notion of (un) structured play for innovation that authors like Wagner (2015) and Stern (2018) adhere to. Rather, the spirit is 'timeless', and as such, it could be cultivated at any time in life, going beyond the limits established by age, institutions or even society.

Such childhood spirit cultivation, according to Droit (2018), involves distilling some key elements for reflection. There is a continuous attempt to speak about or articulate that which cannot be fully understood or spoken about. The attempt resurfaces now and again in the presence of forgotten objects or memories which acquire life on their own, and which could have an ability to disrupt coherent, ego-centred or stable narratives we often adopt about ourselves or the world around us.

The spirit attempts to reconcile the world with the written or spoken word, to reconcile ourselves with our historical memories. And doing so to make us aware that as human beings will never be able to fully explain or reason about that which we observe. Because of this, the spirit of childhood acknowledges that the magical never leaves us, and that when we venture to let it flow in our narratives, it could become a source of inspiration for our present time (s). In short, the childhood spirit could help us find or see creativity where neither language, time nor reason do.

A Spirit for Play

A key element for Droit (2018) in the spirit of childhood is that of **play**. Against a current idea of play in Westernised societies (activity for competition), in other contexts (e.g. India) play can be conceived to classify human activity in different realms of life. According to Droit (2018), in India and other Eastern cultures, there is a 'whole' game that the universe is playing, which we as human beings cannot aspire to fully comprehend: it is a game of encountering and dealing with both diversity and commonalities, surprise and predictability, happiness and catastrophe co-existing together and in non-dialectically opposing ways.

There are rules and improvisations. When we play, we manoeuvre between these. And we restart or refresh playing as if it was the first time. Droit (2018) distinguishes between **restart and iteration**. The former supposes having a fresh look at ourselves and what goes on around us; the latter could be us getting 'bored' and lacking curiosity, openness or passion when playing. Refreshing could also lead us to formulate new game rules, abandon games or play new ones.

Furthermore, our daily life activities and roles could be conceived of as games that we continuously play (Droit 2018). Events, objects and memories acquire life of their own, inviting us to let them speak for us. In games and in life and in a forceless way, we always braid reason and emotions, muting with articulating, experiencing wonder with reality checking.

Games could also become our 'reality', allowing us to generate and live by the meanings we draw from them. In this regard Droit (2018) says:

> Tell me what your conception/notion about play is, and I will tell you how *you* define what is to be human, [child], divine, life, the world .... (p. 71, brackets and italics added, my own translation from Spanish edition)

Spiriting play, making it something pervasive and inspiring in our lives as the above ideas suggest, could help us in our efforts to nurture creativity. We could 'refresh' our computer screens when things become too complicated or complex to deal with (Droit 2018). We could always improvise or do otherwise than is expected by ourselves or others. We could wonder, imagine, irrationalise, not-understand, repeat; we could let go of norms, evidences. We could ask again why, what or how:

> To listen to what is said and what is not said. To discern in a tragedy what could be comical. To detect in a deduction what is arbitrary. To feel what is timeless on a specific occasion. To perceive what is human in the inhumane ... navigating against the tide, using but not succumbing to its winds. (Droit 2018, p. 155, my own translation from Spanish edition)

A Spirit of Seriousness

With the above, individual selves could reflect on how we have been nurturing creativity in ourselves and others, with the possibility of restarting or iterating roles or practices. We can also stop, gain some distance, reflect and extract ourselves from our past or present, draw games or rules for our education or our life in general.

We could, as Droit (2018) does, ask ourselves: 'What about ethical principles, laws and the like?' Droit's answer conceives principles as *illusory*. As human beings, we create them to help us deal with or govern that which is incomprehensible or that which always escapes our desire to control what goes on. The best we could do with ethical principles is to think of them as temporary, non-essential game rules that can be reshaped within the next games' iterations.

Distancing, separation from, reflection about or stopping the playing of games can also lead us to acknowledge the existence of **a spirit of seriousness** (Droit 2018). If taken to the extreme (individually or collectively), the spirit of play could become a house wall that we are to avoid crashing into, a boring or even a dangerous house to inhabit all the time for the first time. Too much playfulness or even creativity could result in continuous fragmentation, movement or discontent for individual selves. At some point, we are to 'stop' playing 'children' and play mature selves (Droit 2018). We need to temporarily 'abandon' the house. We are to tolerate ambiguity, live with some 'sh*t' if not accept or manage it (Manson 2016).

For Droit (2018), our lives could involve moving between the above two poles so that their imbalance could be maintained. Spirits of play and seriousness could help individual selves make more sense of our challenges and possibilities to govern ourselves and others. We can infuse our attitudes, roles and practices with restarting, wonder, humorous and endless efforts to articulate, write or speak about what goes on with ourselves or others. We would need to restore the imbalance by adopting seriousness: stopping, reflecting and accepting reality (also with humour, wisdom or grace). We can 'exist' in the yesterday, the tomorrow and the now, using the gaps in between as a source of creativity and reflection. Droit says:

> The good use of the spirit of childhood [and maturity] means to maintain that imbalance…disturbing the spoken word with silence, silence for the word, the logical for the illogical, the meaningful for the meaningless, seriousness for games, emotions for soberness, stillness for movement, time for eternity, self with the outside. (Droit 2018, p. 153)

With the spirits of play and seriousness together, we could live with **a new systemic paradox**, a more palatable one from that of being part of wholes whilst having to gain their membership: a paradox of being playful whilst also being serious in our dealings with ourselves and the 'wholes' we are part of. This paradox could be also used to inhabit or leave the systemic space for selves proposed earlier. Some implications of this paradox in the use of methods to enquire about creativity are discussed as follows.

Implications for Enquiring About Creativity

In the penultimate section of this chapter, a brief review of several methods that could be used to develop educational inquiries about creativity is presented, and some implications for their use when enquiring about creativity in a playful/serious way are drawn. This review also aims to rediscover creativity inquiry methods in the light of the soft tyrannies presented earlier and the opportunities to use them in the systemic space proposed for selves in management education.

Life Stories

A life story is a fairly complete narrating of one's entire experience of life as a whole, highlighting the most important aspects. (Atkinson 1998, p. 8, original italics)

With the spirit of play, the sort of 'totality' that creativity research methods aim to achieve in the form of defensible accounts, theories or systems models could also include ambivalences, transgressions, incomplete/intermediary, (in)complete ideas, elements, projects or enterprises. There could be play/seriousness in such a totality: presence or absence, silence or noise, isolation or community, certainty or uncertainty, happiness or sadness, achievement or failure, clarity or confusion.

Life stories or idea stories could be playfully written about with a sense of humour as well as seriousness: *as if we were staring at the face of reality with a (tragic) smile and for the first time.* In such stories, there could have been different roles and practices for us or others. We could have experienced a sense of oneness/fragmentation with something bigger than ourselves, or we could guess if or how creativity was (is) or was (is) not present. We could have played or stopped playing with creativity, or vice-versa. In living/imagining the present about ourselves or others, we could keep ourselves and others safe and sane whilst we playfully engage with (or abandon) the tyrannies that pursue knowledge about creativity in management education.

Idea Biographies

From a traditional perspective, the locus of creativity is thought to lie within the individual. From a more systems-based perspective, this same concept becomes socially rearranged and literally redistributed: individuals enact their agency throughout the creative idea development process, but no one individual or group has ownership over any one creative idea. (Clapp 2017, pp. 91–92)

For Clapp (2017), it is possible to change the focus of analysis when enquiring about creativity in education. Shifting from an individual to networks or groups of them, Clapp (2017) argues, richer accounts or analysis can be elaborated. Other actors contributing to or being influenced by the work of lone 'geniuses' can be drawn into narratives.

A key implication of using the idea biography method for educational enquiry (including its evaluation) that Clapp (2017) proposes is that those studying or developing creativity are to consider how 'their actions or [those of others] are always to be socially and culturally situated, and that the greatness they may one day experience will be the result of their own efforts combined with —and amplified by—the distributed efforts of others' (p. 69, brackets added). With the above, Clapp (2017) also considers that power is currently favouring students who are aware of how to use it to become or imitate 'enlarged' individuals. According to him, an epistemological change of focus could bring about awareness of challenges and effects for creativity as a co-construction.

This seems to be a serious and idea-focused position about creativity education, one which could benefit from being a bit more playful, ambivalent or dual as previously mentioned. With the spirit of play/seriousness presented earlier in this chapter, it might be possible as well as desirable to venture to explore creativity, but also iterate to learn about and challenge (non) participatory mindsets and cultures in which selves create. The 'wickedness' that Clapp (2017) argues that creativity often has could be better analysed, this time from the vantage point of game rules or principles that could be reviewed or changed for the benefit of individual selves and others when operating within soft tyrannies.

Concluding Remarks

This chapter has laid out the main features of a spirit of play (and seriousness). It was argued that such a spirit could be valuable to help individual selves enquire about themselves or others as creators living in the present time, whilst imagining other ways of doing so as Foucault's governmentality suggests.

The spirit of play invites us to continuously seek playfulness in what we do or who we think we are. We are to use it as a source of narrative, creativity or reflection. With this spirit, we are to care for ourselves and others whilst we safely inhabit it. In our narratives or enquiries about creativity, we could identify knowledge (rules) of games that we play(ed), or games that we are played at.

And following Droit (2018), we are to balance the spirit of play with a spirit of seriousness for ourselves and others, something that is necessary to also survive the soft tyrannies in management education. This might entail swapping between individual and collective roles/practices, as well as stopping being creative. With these possibilities, to both temporarily inhabit the space for individual selves and abandon it in **what constitutes a new and more palatable paradox: dealing with playfulness/seriousness**. This paradox could make us feel a little bit more as well as less in meaningful control of our creativities, accepting their unfolding as not only the result of our own doings in the light of soft tyrannies, and helping us survive the latter.

In the next chapters of this book, narratives related to creativity and using the above methods are presented. The enquiries undertaken will also provide insights and rules about how individual selves like myself could play with (and be serious about) creativity to (re)discover it. The following is a prelude of what is to come.

A Prelude

What started as a timid way of sharing toys with my neighbour Camilo (I was 7 years old at the time) became the best part of the day. Going to Camilo and Fancho (another friend)'s houses, playing in our back gardens and riding tricycles or pedal cars was the highlight day after day. And then we became explorers of our neighbourhood, gaining friends along the way (Marta, Monica), cycling. I can honestly say that we did that freely, without any prejudices.

I still think that creativity, that magic 'thing' that made us play during that and other summers, was there despite us not seeing it. The best stuff has been the unplanned, the adventurous, the unspeakable, the mysterious.

There was also other stuff that made me grow up without me fully realising it. Camilo's mum died from a strange, indescribable illness shortly after I met him. I remember her tenderness when she cleaned my knee after getting hurt.

After this event, Camilo and his family moved to another city.

Fancho, Marta, the Diegos, Mauricio and I would go on to develop a long friendship, sometimes relying on each other at university or parties. We would stay overnight studying and listening to music. We would organise dancing parties, sing in Christmas or Sunday mass choirs, go to a farm or cycling, I would crash my family cars in one of their houses. We would be told off by our parents.

And with other bereavements, we would stay close to each other. Don't ask me if or how we keep in touch. We just do.

A rule for creativity and life: *Look after friendships!*

References

Atkinson, R. (1998). *The Life Story Interview.* Sage University Papers Series on Qualitative Research Methods. Thousand Oaks: Sage.

Barros-Castro, R., Córdoba-Pachón, J. R., & Pinzón-Salcedo, L. (2014). A Systemic Framework for Evaluating Computer-Supported Collaborative Learning—Mathematical Problem-solving (CSCL-MPS) Initiatives: Insights from a Colombian Case. *Systemic Practice and Action Research, 27,* 265–285.

Bateson, M. C. (1994). *Peripheral Visions: Learning Along the Way.* New York: Harper.

Berg, M., & Seeber, B. (2016). *The Slow Professor: Challenging the Culture of Speed in the Academy.* Toronto: University of Toronto Press.

Cain, S. (2013). *Quiet: The Power of Introverts in a World That Can't Stop Talking.* New York: Penguin.

Clapp, E. (2017). *Participatory Creativity: Introducing Access to Equity to the Creative Classroom.* New York: Routledge.

Córdoba-Pachón, J. R. (2007). A critical Systems View of Power-Ethics Interactions in Information Systems Evaluation. *Information Resources Management Journal, 20*(2), 74–89.

Córdoba-Pachón, J. R. (2010). *Systems Practice in the Information Society.* London: Routledge.

Córdoba-Pachón, J. R. (2019). *Managing Creativity: A Systems Thinking Journey.* London: Routledge.

Craft, A. (2013). Childhood, Possibility Thinking and Wise, Humanising Educational Futures. *International Journal of Educational Research, 61,* 126–134.

Droit, J. P. (2018). *Volver a ser Niño: Experiencias de Filosofía* (trans: Núria Petit Fontserè). Spain: Ediciones Paidós.

Glavenau, V. (2010). Principles for a Cultural Psychology of Creativity. *Culture & Psychology, 16*(2), 147–163. https://doi.org/10.1177/1354067X10361394.

Manson, M. (2016). *The Subtle Art of Not Giving a Fuck - A Counter-Intuitive Approach to Living a Good Life*. New York: HarperOne.

Rose, E. (2013). *On Reflection: An Essay on Technology, Education and the Status of Thought in the Twenty-First Century*. Toronto: Canadian Scholars' Press Inc.

Stern, A. (2018). Tous Enthousiastes! Retrouvez Votre Énergie d'Enfant. Paris: Editions Horay.

Vygotsky, L. S. (1979). *Mind in Society: The Development of Higher Psychological Processes* (2nd ed.). Cambridge, MA: Harvard University Press.

Wagner, T. (2015). *Creating Innovators: The Making of Young People Who Will Change the World*. New York: Scribner, Simon and Schuster, Inc.

CHAPTER 6

First Rediscoveries of Creativity

Introduction

A psychotherapist said to me that I grew up fearing that which I perceived as inadequate. I also feared rejection or separation from 'clans': close family and friends, organisations or movements I joined. My life memories of coping with the first issue whilst being part of the second are currently blurred. All I can say now about these memories is that I have survived, and I am here, so is my creativity(ies). It is still difficult for me though to acknowledge and deal with failure as mentioned in the introduction of this book.

Inspired in the spirit of play (and seriousness), this chapter depicts narratives of what I call my first encounters with creativity. In those I refresh my own memories, recognise the surfacing and presence of different selves of mine. These narratives are short life stories that depict events and objects revisited when playing a game that I call **hide and seek** with creativity (Fig. 6.1) and which I can see selves and practices surface.

I distinguish 'assigned' roles of child, Catholic family member or friend, student. There are moments of curiosity, fear, anxiety, fun, hope, inspiration sadness or 'wonder' in which I guess where creativity is as a muse and she also tries to find me (Gilbert 2015). Through practices like reading, (type)writing and reflecting, meditation, socialising, then and now, I could experience both wonder and timelessness, I try to articulate again what goes on or make sense of who I was and am.

Figure 6.1 shows a 'time' map of the perhaps non-linear and vague paths, turns and twists of the game. Creativity kept hidden and only appeared

© The Author(s) 2020
J.-R. Córdoba-Pachón, *Creativity in Management Education*,
https://doi.org/10.1007/978-3-030-50960-6_6

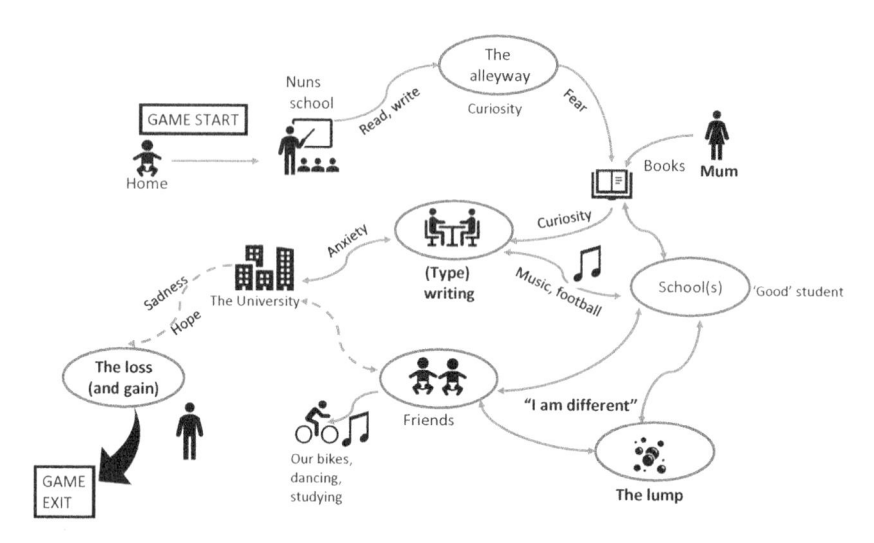

Fig. 6.1 A map of a hide and seek game

occasionally, paradoxically. She hid behind some reassuring objects (books, typewriter) and moments (with friends, a course on systems thinking, a good mentor or boss) to awaken my desires. Embedded in narratives I set out some rules, which I want to share with the reader. At the end of the chapter, I exit the game and provide further reflections from adopting a spirit of seriousness about my selves and creativity which could have important implications for education.

In distinguishing different selves of mine, I am inspired by the possibilities laid out previously for individual selves in the previous chapter of this book. We could practise things like writing/reading, learning, meditating, we could reflect (via mindfulness meditation or other practices) on our feelings, illusions or limits that we attribute to ourselves as individuals (Wright, 2017). We could also decide to be serious about them, and practise to 'let go' of some.

The Alleyway

My first schooling was at a kindergarten. Located at the other end of the same street where we lived, it was run by Catholic nuns. Both strict and warm, one of them taught me to read at a very early age. I had to wear uniform.

I enjoyed reading and writing, and my mother also encouraged me to do so; I do not remember exactly how I learned. I can only remember the joy of having experienced a kind of 'aha' moment, where all the pieces of the puzzle came together. And then the praise of teachers and everyone else. First time I think I could find creativity (or she could find me).

The joy and curiosity that followed were also mixed with fear. One day my good friend and I ventured to go out at the back of one of the classrooms, only to find we were staring at one of the nuns in the toilet through the toilet's window. She shouted, and the nuns and kids were ordered by her to block and lock the entrance to the alleyway. I remember kids grabbing and throwing sand at us and building a barricade to stop us escaping. Luckily, we did in time, but were punished and had to stay outside the classroom for a while.

My caricaturised smile in Fig. 6.2 reflects joy and fear of learning at an early age, not only how to meet what was required, but also how to escape the vigilance of my teachers. I guess creativity was peeking at me and my friend through the toilet window and staring curiously, as if the best/worst was to come. I can also see her looking at my hands when the nuns 'arranged' my posture for the picture. The game instilled in me a sense of loyalty to my friends whilst creativity prayed with me that I could understand what was going on so that I did not get hurt in the process.

Fig. 6.2 A kindergarten picture

1975

Rule
- When venturing down an alleyway to seek creativity, always bring a friend 😊

(Type)writing

The old typewriter was and is still sitting there, waiting to be used. I can recall memories of using it. Together with a printed encyclopaedia, my mum's, and other books received on birthdays, my grandfather and father's typewriters helped me write and dream.

I started first by typing some practical exercises from a manual that somebody had left in our home: my elder brothers and sister were already doing this. Then, and using the encyclopaedia, I wrote some of my high school homework. Time stops and leaps, and I find myself typewriting on a computer that my mum, 'the mother', bought for me when I started studying computer science and systems engineering. At other times used by others at home, it also became part of my software programming, studying or working routines. It was now the 1990s.

With these typewriters I became a writing self, a busy self, a creative self, also a perfectionist-anxious self who wanted to see the result of my writing straight away. The typewriter became a tool for group work and even for helping my dad write his legal documents. With an internship and the end of my university degree, I forgot about this new typewriter. It sat there, silently, waiting for the next assignment to come. It also became quickly outdated. Being moved to a new family business facility that me and my brothers set up, it got stolen. Robbers came and left through the roof on a weekend with it.

For me, the typewriter stored letters, essays, programmes, lawsuits or writings of when I was trying to become an adult. Ink rolls or electronic memories recorded adventures and misadventures. Deleting and erasing them is never easy, because the typewriter, like the spirit of play, still asks me to go back and correct, to refresh or to start anew (Droit 2018). It feels good when a new 'page' starts. I still remember the wonder and awe experienced when completing a task, or the frustration and anxiety of having to amend, classify, recover or restart.

Rule

- **With some meaningful practices (i.e. reading, writing), we could play to experience wonder, timelessness or 'refresh' our ideas about ourselves and others.**

When I look at the above Fig. 6.3, I also see myself as a 'saviour' on a mission to help the world. The Catholic nuns should have also included a sacred history book that my great auntie 'Galle' gave me. For some time, I pictured myself as one of the Old Testament kings, doing good for his people. A saviour self, a worried, perfectionist-anxious one writing too.

Creativity could have been hiding inside the typewriter's machinery. She could have waited for me to go to sleep to look at the pages that I wrote and the mistakes I made. In my dreams, she could have murmured something for me to try to articulate the next day. Creativity could have been hiding in my father and my grandfather's writings too, as she does in my twin sister and my mum's when I typewrite miles away from them.

With reading and writing, I am playing to catch up with, or fully articulate or control reality. Always an incomplete and irrational magical experience that leaves me in wonder or anxiety. A governing technology, one encapsulated in creativity concepts like 'flow' (Csikszentmihalyi 1996), one that I have been able to use to rediscover different selves without using such concepts too much or too explicitly. I just play.

Fig. 6.3 Typewriter (s)

With the typewriters, I (could) extract myself though, become someone else. I could be my son when he wants to touch and explore, when he asks questions about how things work. I could also be a perfectionist-anxious adult when trying to write correctly, and when getting frustrated by not doing so. I could be my daughter when she writes on the kitchen board, and I could be my wife when she asks me to help with sentences for her work or blog posts on science fiction books and novels. I could be the educator I currently am. Time stops and leaps again.

Rule
- **As a creator, just read, write or do anything that makes you experience awe, wonder or even frustration, something you need to live with, something you cannot live without at the time.**

The Lump(s)

I still remember vividly the black lumps on the street nearby our home. A mixture of oil and blood…

At the time of the event, the media talked about one of the hitmen dying there as his head crashed against the pavement when escaping from the minister's bodyguards (Fig. 6.4). A few moments and a hundred

Fig. 6.4 The lump(s)

metres away, he and his accomplice had just gunned down the Colombian Minister of Justice.

This was to become the first of many crimes resulting from the fight against drug cartels in the 1980s and 1990s in the country. I—a teenager—and some friends waited a few days before venturing to see the lump by ourselves. We were curious and nervous. We wanted to see how spectacular the killing of both the good and bad guys had been.

For friends like Fancho, Diego, Mauricio, Marthica and the 'garnapias', this was a different adventure from our cowboys and Indians games, dancing, throwing stones at cars and running away, cycling or from competing among ourselves. **This was serious.**

Looking at the lump(s) made me feel different. There was play and there was also horrific play. The good and bad guys were real. Looking back, I wanted to quit the hide and seek game. The spirit of seriousness settled, albeit temporarily. I keep saying to my UK and Colombian students that they are seriously lucky to be (alive) and at university.

Rule
- **There are good guys and bad guys in life.**

Today I sometimes feel like an impostor when I see life just disappear or when it becomes something else than planned. When this happens, my perfectionist-anxious self, that which got accepted at school as a 'good student', takes over to berate failings or to value the present. Other selves (hard-working, sensitive, thoughtful, self-aware, religious) take a back seat. This perfectionist-anxious self can invite others (jealous, pessimistic) to join the party, only to discover how lucky I am.

It is in these and other moments and paradoxically, as individuals we could also seek creativity. With the spirit of play and seriousness, we could accept or acknowledge that there are some 'sh*t' things that just are in our lives (Manson 2016). We had better accept and deal with them, rather than trying to rationally deny, explain or analyse them. Let us be grateful, let us restart.

Rule
- **Sometimes, life is hard…and this could be a good, lucky thing.**

The University

On a Friday afternoon, the last day for student university registration, I finally decide to tell my parents what I want to study at university: computer science and systems engineering. I notice my father's desperation. He would have been restraining himself from yelling at me or telling me what to do.

I had been accepted at five (5) different universities. Although engineering sounded interesting and I had confidence in myself, somehow, I was not fully thrilled. Moreover, I did not want to be a financial burden to my parents because I was to go to a private university, the best but most expensive in the country at the time.

After talking to one of my brothers and my mum's friends who said, 'What is money for if not for spending it on our children's future?', I give in and sign up for engineering. And I do so against a careers counsellor who advises I should study law, and with some fear and anxiety.

I am to study in a non-familiar, expensive and competitive environment. My parents would happily approve to pay only ten (10) semesters. Thanks to their encouragement and assertiveness, and my grandfather and his inheritance (including the typewriter!), I am now able to write books like this.

Rule (Extended from Gilbert 2015)
- **Be grateful (to your parents and grandparents, siblings, friends and mentors), always.**

In the late 1980s in Colombia, there was already a clear distinction between knowledge disciplines like engineering and law that had been inherited from colonial times, and which seemed to follow global trends and tensions between education and professionalisation of public and private workers (Lundgreen 1990; Safford 2014). The Spanish culture that we as Colombians inherited had made emphasis on humanities privileging public service careers, and somehow dismissed the more technical or commercially oriented ones. My grandfather had been a lawyer, and so was my father. My twin sister Claudia decided she was also going to be (another reason for me to do something different).

Since the nineteenth century any effort to modernise or professionalise education in Colombia has assumed a direct link with economic development, something that has not been always the case elsewhere. According to Lundgreen (1990), European and US governments followed different trajectories in relation to the education of their public bureaucracies and the emergence of the commercial bourgeoisie. In the nineteenth century the education of these cadres was not initially driven by universities, but rather by specialised schools to train the engineering elites (civil servants) vis-à-vis other elites (lawyers). In countries like the UK and later the US, workshop and shop floor education was conceived of as separate and not leading to professionalisation.

Only when economic markets went beyond countries' territories and from the end of the nineteenth century onwards, did established universities in France, Germany, the UK and the US take an interest in hosting technically oriented engineering schools and doing so with a liberal orientation for education, so that engineers would also learn abstract thinking (i.e. maths). Networking and other forms of socialisation (i.e. professional associations and accreditations) contributed later to professionalise engineering education (Lundgreen 1990).

In Colombia after independence from Spanish rule in 1819 (Safford 2014), new governments aimed to emulate the success of other countries like the UK and the US. Aiming to differentiate Colombia from its colonisers, they embarked on different educational efforts to 'modernise' it. What was not that clear at the time, according to Safford (2014), was that Colombia had different environmental conditions for education than those of the countries they wanted to emulate: a difficult geography and a very small market.

Efforts to professionalise engineering in the nineteenth century in Colombia were scarce and directed towards sending students abroad (Ibid). In a similar way to some developed countries, engineering education started with the army (bridge construction, civil engineering) and gained momentum with the establishment of professional associations. The National University of Colombia set up a school of engineering in the early 1900s (Torres-Sánchez and Salazar-Hurtado 2002; Safford 2014). It was only in the late 1940s that private universities like the one I chose followed.

My alma mater for computer science and systems engineering followed a US-based style of education which enabled students to study a major and choose other options (courses, minors). Despite this degree of freedom, individualism and competition, soothed by a liberal arts style of education, taking on big challenges and proving oneself by doing so, became part of the culture I studied in. My perfectionist-anxious self seems to have prevailed on many occasions in this environment in order to help me learn, pass or succeed: at times though, I felt free to explore other, non-technical subjects like history and social psychology, ethics and society, and we could debate issues with our teachers. And my guess is that creativity could have been there to listen, encourage, help and soothe me and the others.

Rule (Extended From McClam and Flores-Scott 2012)
- **Students need to be made more aware of the historical and knowledge circumstances and derived soft tyrannies of the educational institutions they study at. They could be allowed to do and be otherwise than expected. Let us be grateful, let us restart, let us keep moving.**

Prior to entering university, I had been a successful student, but not so much now. I failed some exams and scraped to pass others. I had to start from scratch by consciously and anxiously attending lectures, taking notes, reading consciously, doing exercises, staying overnight alone or with group mates, waking up early to prepare for assignments and examinations. And I was part of a family that liked social engagements, and I also liked some of them.

In moments of anxiety or frustration, creativity could have been there: in the classroom, in lectures unrelated to engineering, the university library or at home all the time. Sitting quietly, holding my hand and listening, suffering when I self-berated, and happier when I passed even though I claimed it was only me who did it. She would also shout at me when I grieved about achieving very good but not perfect overall results.

And I guess that she was also there when I found teachers that I liked, and with some of my close friends or companions. Together, we made life more fun. We also played football, danced in homemade parties, cycled to nearby towns, or stayed up until dawn learning physics or statistics.

During university, I joined a 'mini-crusade' Catholic movement elsewhere, in which I became absorbed in promoting change in the world by changing ourselves. I partied, I fell in love, I got girlfriends, I got heartbroken. I enjoyed and survived some social engagements.

It was also where, through my lecturer Ernesto and his systems thinking course, I think creativity whispered into my ear: 'I am excited!' In this course I would enjoy looking at systems models of activity, visiting a company that one of my classmates had access to, and then doing an internship on the advice of another. Time stops and leaps again, and here I am writing another book on systems thinking and creativity.

When I went back to finish my engineering degree after my internship at Colmena savings and loans corporation, I felt I could still do the technical bits (i.e. programming), but somehow knew I wanted to work in real and complex situations that required interacting with people. Computer-based modelling, systems rich pictures and writing took over from coding deep in my heart. This, despite my best attempts to deny it by taking a software development job months later and realising I could do it, but needed to follow more my inner, playful self.

At university creativity had for me another surprise. After a faculty meeting, I could see that some lecturers took notice of me. Many years later and after graduation, I would visit them to find that despite what I thought, they positively remember(ed) me. Maybe they could see what I had not: a 'good enough' set of selves. A grateful refresh, a re-start of who I was, who I am or could be.

Rule
- **It is OK to wanting to be or do something different. We just need to pay bit more of attention to what goes on in our lives, that which really turns us on. Thankful, always thankful. Let us restart and refresh our creativities.**

I studied, graduated and worked at bigger organisations. In those, I met wonderful bosses and mentors, as well as afraid ones. Through university and industry experience I have learned that **covering the basics** is as important as dreaming of big ideas or projects (more on this lesson later in the book). The spirit of seriousness is there and we as creators had better acknowledge it, returning to it when we find difficulties or when our perfectionist-anxious selves take over. Life was preparing me for accepting the good and not so good.

A Loss

It was a sunny day in August 1996. I remember as I was working at one of my jobs and had to phone the secretary of our relatively new family business. In our conversation, I asked her to phone my brother Juan Carlos (he was the business salesman) so he could phone one of our clients. I was angry at him. After getting a call from the secretary, Juan Carlos would look for a public payphone and join the queue to phone the client. Before him in the queue there was a drug dealer who would be shot at by a passer-by in a motorcycle in no time. In the shooting, I lost my brother Juan Carlos in a second. I felt very sad and guilty. I still do sometimes.

I look back at this memory with humility and somehow wonder when writing this. I see my students who are oblivious to these memories. They have been born elsewhere and are facing other life issues, perhaps less related to personal safety. Me and them, we are anxious, as I was on those days, as I am often now, seeking refuge at university. Occasionally I tell them my life story and this episode to highlight how it made me rethink who I thought I was at the time and who I could be. Grateful, always grateful please.

Rule (Extended from Above)
- **Sometimes, life is hard *and sad*. And that could *also* be an opportunity, a wakeup call.**

Exiting the Game: Serious Reflections

After my brother Juan Carlos died, I got better at guessing where creativity was. She tried to soothe my feelings of sadness and guilt. Funnily enough, she also encouraged me to not only play my social roles, please my loved ones, my friends or colleagues circles or even my family or home country.

I went abroad to study and an opportunity to continue doing social science research found me. As I travelled back temporarily, and on the encouragement of my brother Ricardo, I decided to have several psychotherapy and later counselling sessions. Through those, I started realising that I could not be physically or emotionally in two different geographical contexts at the same time. I have also realised the existence of my perfectionist-anxious self and a tendency to please people, live by their opinions and/or rise above them with hard and silent work at what I was good at: reading and writing.

Finishing my studies abroad and continuing a different (educational) career path has proved and still proves to be challenging, whilst also rewarding in ways I did not expect. There is individual hard work to be put in everywhere to learn and re-learn the basics of something. And with it, there is a temptation for me to often become a perfectionist-anxious self to the detriment of my other selves (caring, thoughtful, organised, serious, chilled, self-compassionate, etc.).

I have been fortunate enough to get support along the way. Sometimes this support has been available at university. Support is also an incomplete governing enterprise. I can reveal some and keep other individual, private selves and practices from public view. Creativity could be noticed in those moments when I enter and leave the house of play, often with the support or encouragement of other people.

Rule
- For creativity, our different selves (i.e. **perfectionist-anxious**) would need to be accepted and balanced with other selves (curious, adventurous, organised, humorous, loving). Support is important.

I am now **accepting** this perfectionist-anxious self a bit more and with difficulty. Other practices like mindfulness meditation and well-being activities (crafting, drawing, walking, cycling among others) have helped me recognise and manage some of the triggers that bring it to the surface: overwork, a sense of failure (more on this later in the book), competition, jealousy, financial worries, family conflicts. When any of these happen, I retreat, I become silent and irritable, creativity leaves me, I leave the house of the spirit of play.

After some self-berating, feeling guilty, having some time for reflection and rest, reaching out for help, I strive to adopt what I think is a spirit of calm seriousness. I count my blessings; I organise things, I go to the cinema, watch TV, I enjoy bit of junk food or a shopping treat. I attend my well-being groups to gain strength to say no in the future.

I swim or cycle if not walk around. And I talk to my wife and good friends like Cecilia, John and Adrian. I plead self-compassion (more on this in the next chapter of this book) and review what I want to do in my life and who I want to be: **an ok, good enough guy**.

And all of the above could also become an opportunity to let our creativities flow, and for ourselves to become bit more systemic with them. It is also important to challenge, if not contribute to transform, educational environments and their derived soft tyrannies where some of us contribute to scare our creativity. Spaces for recovery, rest, solitary reflection (and unlinked to action) are much needed if management education is to continue.

Partly in line with what Rose (2013) and Craft (2013) advocate, perhaps it is now time to use our creativity to imagine other ways (individual, collective) of learning. Information and communication technologies or ICTs could be used to foster new ways of thinking or interacting in education, not only enabling timely interaction for monitoring or assessment of students. As I reflect upon in the last chapter of this book, we might think of new ways of bringing education to each other, respecting our individual selves and developing other and more compassionately collective forms of education. In the midst of situations like those derived by the world pandemic, creativity could help us to imagine our lives in simpler and more humane ways.

Concluding Remarks

This chapter has narrated a game called hide and seek with creativity in my life. Through short life stories, it has been shown that individual selves could assume different socially or individually oriented roles. In my case, my student roles were supported by being a member of certain 'clans': close friends and family, my alma mater, my home country. As individuals, we could accept the existence of these roles, even if what we think is creativity might not show herself when (un)consciously adopting them.

Through reading, writing, accepting and reflecting on these narratives I have been able to acknowledge the surfacing of different selves: perfectionist-anxious, hard-working, conscious, organised, thoughtful, socially oriented and calm among others. I have been fortunate to experience a sense of wonder of and connection with something bigger. I have lost myself and experienced wonder or frustration. Other practices like meditation, chilling out, therapy and well-being have helped me acknowledge the importance of accepting selves, roles and practices, and managing them adequately. I am acknowledging my limitations and opportunities in my life as it has been and as it is now. And this awareness needs also to be extended to my environments.

As mentioned earlier in this book, Wagner (2015) advocates developing a *culture* where creativity can happen: mentors, (un)structured play activities, becoming aware of our passions and purposes in life, could be among other elements to be nurtured. My reflections in this chapter lead me to suggest that educational institutions need to look at themselves more playfully and seriously at the same time. To their history and soft tyrannies which could often focus on promoting individualism, competition, disciplining and economic reward to the detriment of the learning processes lying underneath (Oakley 2014), but which could also be made more compassionate and sensitive to students own circumstances.

Referring to my own case as a student self, it seems the balance was tipped towards (individually competitive and socialisation) knowledge processes than to other forms of self-care or learning (Drummond 2003).

For the future, we as students or educators could better consider who we are so that we can develop new ways of being. And that should be OK with ourselves, our loved ones and our educational institutions.

This chapter also aims to convey a message of hope for the rediscovery of creativity: it is difficult but possible to let other selves flourish. To do so, the following rules or recommendations could be followed:

- Educational degrees do not need to be straightjackets to be followed to the letter.
- Students could be made more aware of the historical and knowledge limits of their educational institutions. But they should not be made fully responsible for acting on them. We could, together, thank for what we have received, somehow laugh at what is going on, and find better ways to relate to each other. Let us restart, refresh.
- Different opportunities for learning and assessment could be kept open and defended from financial pressures, myths and soft tyrannies of economic growth or knowledge disciplining.
- Let us or our management students pursue what we want rather than only what we can or are able to do.
- Let us find ourselves practices that make us experience curiosity and wonder. Let us do so regardless of what our loved ones think or approve.
- Let us recognise those selves that scare the muse of creativity (like perfectionist-anxious ones), let us accept them and manage them.
- Friends, counsellors or therapists are important to help us manage our different selves and practices, to face our fears and venture to go into alleyways.
- Life is serious, mysterious, funny, playful, uncontrollable, let us be grateful for it, let us protect it. *Restart, keep moving.*

References

Craft, A. (2013). Childhood, Possibility Thinking and Wise, Humanising Educational Futures. *International Journal of Educational Research, 61*, 126–134.

Csikszentmihalyi, M. (1996). *Creativity: Flow and the Psychology of Discovery and Invention.* New York: Harper Collins.

Droit, J. P. (2018). *Volver a ser Niño: Experiencias de Filosofía* (trans: Núria Petit Fontserè). Spain: Ediciones Paidós.

Drummond, J. (2003). Care of the Self in a Knowledge Economy: Higher Education, Vocation and the Ethics of Michel Foucault. *Educational Philosophy and Theory, 35*(1), 57–69.
Gilbert, E. (2015). *Big Magic: Creative Living Beyond Fear.* London: Bloomsbury.
Lundgreen, P. (1990). Engineering Education in Europe and the U.S.A., 1750–1930: The Rise to Dominance of School Culture and the Engineering Professions. *Annals of Science, 47*(1), 33–75.
Manson, M. (2016). *The Subtle Art of Not Giving a F*ck. A Counterintuitive Approach to Living a Good Life.* New York: Harper.
McClam, S., & Flores-Scott, E. (2012). Transdisciplinary Teaching and Research: What Is Possible in Higher Education? *Teaching in Higher Education, 17*(3), 231–243.
Oakley, B. (2014). *A Mind for Numbers.* Tarcher/Putnam: New York.
Rose, E. (2013). *On Reflection: An Essay on Technology, Education, and the Status of Thought in the Twenty-First Century.* Toronto: Canadian Scholars Press Inc.
Safford, F. (2014). *El Ideal de lo Práctico: El Desafío de Formar una Élite Técnica y Empresarial en Colombia.* Medellín: Fondo Editorial Universidad EAFIT. Segunda Edición.
Torres-Sánchez, J., & Salazar-Hurtado, L. A. (2002). In Universidad Nacional de Colombia (Ed.), *Introducción a la Historia de la Ingeniería y la Educación en Colombia.* Bogotá: Unibiblos.
Wagner, T. (2015). *Creating Innovators: The Making of Young People Who Will Change the World.* New York: Scribner, Simon and Schuster, Inc.
Wright, R. (2017). *Why Buddhism Is True – The Science and Philosophy of Meditation and Enlightenment.* New York: Simon and Schuster.

CHAPTER 7

Taking Creativity to the Classroom

INTRODUCTION

From the previous chapter and in different forms (objects, events, rules), creativity has become a dear friend of mine rather than a muse. In our previous game of hide and seek, I have been able to recognise valuable old selves and practices, and I have been able to manage if not 'survive' the influence of collective 'clans' and roles whilst developing my individual/public creativity. I have also acknowledged the existence of a perfectionist-anxious self. This one seems to emerge when I am (self) drawn to collective and often impossible demands, one of them being 'saving the world'.

In this chapter and through short narratives oriented towards idea stories (Clapp 2017), I narrate both refreshing(s), re-starts **and** iterations of a game called 'Let us protect our most precious selves'. The difference between refreshing(s) and iterations is that in the former I try to play as if it was for the first time.

A key lesson from this chapter is that creativity and I—now friends—must make sure that we do not get 'killed' in the classroom via the operation of soft tyrannies in management education. To do so we would need to be both playful and serious (i.e. exploring alleyways, organising, failing, stopping, reflecting, saying no), acknowledging also our perennial nature as beings.

The chapter is organised as follows. I present a glimpse of the narratives I want to articulate in the chapter in the form of a picture with courts, refreshing(s) and iterations. I then narrate in more depth my experiences when nurturing creativity using some of the nurturing ideas and perspectives previously described in chapter 3 of this book. In some situations, I find it difficult but not impossible to fail. This could lead me to laugh more often about my different selves (i.e. anxious-perfectionist) when playing, and to be bit more mystical-realistic about life in general (Droit 2018). In a more serious one, the above leads me to reconsider saying no and be more (self) compassionate to laugh a bit more about what goes on.

A GAME IN TWO COURTS

Figure 7.1 shows a glimpse of how I and my students have played with creativity in management education in the last few years. I can distinguish two 'courts' in which I have played the game of protecting our most precious selves, using governmentality and the spirit of play ideas presented previously in this book. (A) My attempts to generate systemic awareness about sustainability have taken the specific form of looking at the phenomena of **recycling**. And (B) I have also been asked to play the game of **learning numbers**. In each court there are several iterations of the game that were/are being played by myself and my friend creativity.

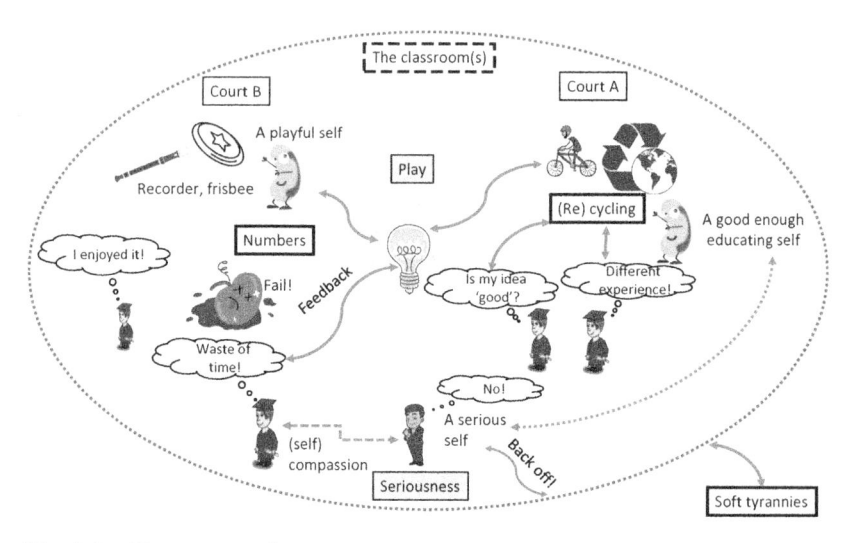

Fig. 7.1 Two courts of a new game

A Refreshing: Slowly (Re)recycling

After some deliberation with myself, and a bit of frowning from loved ones, I have bought myself an electric bike or e-bike.

To make storage space, I sold my recycled bike. The person who acquired it said, 'It is a bargain!', after me trying to explain all the things that this 'old vintage' bike had, including my loyalty to it and what it represents: a recycled self—someone who decided to cycle again and regained pleasure in getting bikes gradually fixed. A bit of my current recycling enthusiastic me went with the sold bike.

But an old one resurfaced: that teenager who used to cycle around the neighbourhood never wearing a helmet, competing once to find out that it was too hard to do so, falling over a few times and crying in front of friends. The one dreaming about fellow Colombian cyclists climbing in Europe, the one who lost the bike that mum bought on credit and specially for him, the one who re-painted or repaired a couple of old bikes when arriving in the UK. I am now an old self, going down alleyways (this time alone), rediscovering some curiosity and passion (Wagner 2015).

With the e-bike I have now found myself doing bits of riding with my children and struggling to decide how to include cycling in mid-life. I have also found myself getting excited when explaining to students and colleagues, what an e-bike does, and how I use it. In the company of creativity and after being convinced by the enthusiastic Steve who sold me an electric bike, I begin to 'pedal' slowly; I keep a good posture; I take time to prepare the bike equipment (battery, clothing, lighting, work documents, lock) before setting off. I do not venture too far on my own or with my children. I am slowly learning to start every day of cycling as a new day, to be patient and to enjoy being 'slow', something that challenges the old and perfectionist ones elicited in the last chapter of this book and elsewhere (Córdoba-Pachón 2019).

Having done mindfulness meditation for the last few years (sometimes frequently, some other times when I feel anxious), often I catch myself in a speedy mode which gets reinforced by the 'lack of time' function of soft tyrannies. I want to do many things in class and with my research; I dream of wonderful ideas when showering, walking or going to bed. I feel worried about my job, my families, our future. The perfectionist-anxious self from the last chapter takes over and makes me 'speed up'.

I know I need to let these feelings pass. In this game of protecting what I consider my best selves (calm, noble, organised, inventive, enthusiastic, etc), the perfectionist-anxious self plays back by arguing that I need to be more creative and that creativity is now my 'field of knowledge': I need to show this in my research and teaching. In the space that I create for all these selves and within soft tyrannies, I know that this latter argument is just an illusion, something that can be let go as part of my different selves (Wright 2017). Still, the game continues. Life continues. New iterations of the game happen. I like my job, at least some parts of it where I can be creative and encourage others. I feel grateful.

After a few journeys to and back from work during spring and summer on the new e-bike, and some clashes with myself and others (drivers, my wife, students), I am (re)learning a few **rules** to play with the power functions of lack of time and knowledge disciplining:

Rules
- I am not that physically young anymore, and the 'roads' (physical, emotional) are bumpy; following my passion and curiosity needs grounding in who I am now (father, academic, still foreigner);
- Cycling, or 'learning' and dealing with creativity involves 'slowness' (Berg and Seeber 2016). **Extension**: even if one tries to follow the rhythm of other cyclists (colleagues) or races (institutions);
- To follow 'safety' practices, wear helmet and visible clothing. I need to rest at times, mindfully meditate, humour, walk, to express my feelings, say no whenever possible, look after my own well-being (Córdoba-Pachón 2019);
- Contributing to saving the planet by reducing car pollution is not an easy business, as many of us still want to be fast to close the gaps between ourselves and reality as we see it. Let us not panic. The world is more complex and interconnected than we can fully understand. And the coronavirus has reminded us all of this.

As Bateson (1994) says, this 'cycling' self is combining the old and the new, it is beginning to converse and interact with others in its adaptation to new situations. I am learning that I don't need to show to others how and radically 'creative' or 'adventurous' I am, at least not all the time. I just need to enjoy this type of 'small' creativity as a collective role or use of my individual roles and activities to teach my students. In this game, safety means seriousness and vice-versa.

I say after a tiring cycling journey: I have to accept that easy does it. Creativity, my friend, munches her sandwich and shouts: "I told you so! One step at a time, (re)learn to walk AND cycle before you run".

I reply: "No you did not, you were all up for enthusiasm, asking me to be a lone creative genius, perfect and save the world, remember?"

After some silence and reflection from both parties, we call it quits. For now.

An Iteration: Recycling and Digital Innovation

The above cycling experience and rules have also influenced my teaching of creativity elsewhere. I am more mindful of my new selves, some of which have been 'buried' and are waiting to be reborn. I teach with passion how the brain works and how we need to train our brain to chunk information, recall it and put it in practice (Oakley 2014). I am also more aware and less fearful of engaging with my physical and social surroundings (Bateson 1994).

Having seen how student residences on our university campus are left during summer and in between student intakes for each year, I set up a student assignment in my final year undergraduate course of digital innovation management. In this written assignment, my students are asked to identify needs for recycling specific items (clothes, electronics, plastics, furniture, etc.) and generate digital solutions to improve recycling processes. To do well in their assignments, I repeatedly encourage my students to go out and speak to different stakeholders, to generate and validate a storyboard and business plan for their solutions, to also engage with their surroundings, to challenge their assumptions (Montuori 2012). This whilst I contact our university estates manager who I heard talking about plans to increase the total percentage of waste that is recycled on campus (including student residences).

Arriving a bit late for one of my classes of this course (now delivered online because of the coronavirus situation), creativity and I have an epiphany. The spirit of play visits and makes me leap on time, mute in wonder, and I try to articulate what comes to mind: taking on a new course, talking about recycling to students, setting up what I think is a creative assessment and using creativity criteria to mark it (Cropley and Cropley 2016). I remember students asking me if their idea for a digital innovation or solution to recycle is 'good' or not and becoming impatient with their endless questions and wrong interpretations about the assignment, their understandings of the increasing returns offered by digital technologies and their worries about their exams. Wow, a lot has gone on.

The perfectionist-anxious self surfaces, arguing that it is my fault for not clearly explaining to my students. At home, my wife helps me calm down and enjoy being online as well as valuing my creativity.

Rule
- There are always many good things in what we do as management educators in creativity.

An Iteration: Diverging and Converging in Bike Recycling

By the time I get to teach second year undergraduate management students, they know how to play the games derived from the emerging function of 'lack of time'. Most of them know what is required in terms of lectures, group activities, assignments, exams, committees, unions, feedback, attendance and so on. Their attendance diminishes, and I hope it is also because they are rediscovering themselves.

In parallel with the above recycling iterations, I set up another assignment where students are to become familiarised with bicycle recycling processes. They are to propose meaningful improvements to a chosen bike recycling process or set of processes. Students are taught and encouraged to use divergent and convergent creativity thinking techniques like the rich picture, random word, concept fan, or cost benefit analysis. They can also incorporate some business process management philosophies (design thinking, complexity thinking, creativity at work, etc.) to justify their proposed solutions.

Last year, students and I were able to visit a bicycle recycling facility nearby. The project manager was very kind, prepared a very informative flyer, explained it and let us see how they work. The visit proved to be novel. I think students got a good impression of how it is to work with different goals and pressures in mind in organisations like this (i.e. be profitable whilst contributing to sustainability and quality of life improvements). I felt very satisfied by having developed this idea. For me this experience meant going back to what I like to do as an educator, which is to put students in touch (again) with their local surroundings (Córdoba-Pachón and Campbell 2008). It also meant going back to some of my old 'saviour' self: using my skills, knowledge and willingness to help others.

This time the saviour-self did not overdo it as a perfectionist-anxious one. He teamed up with creativity for the benefit of the students. He let others (managers) take part in creativity.

In that year, I also encouraged students to help me draft a report with our insights to give to the facility manager. We worked together, I compiled ideas and made the report. I sent it and went for a quick visit afterwards to follow it up with the manager. He said he gave the report to their boss, they said it was useful...

Rule
- Creative educators and students, we made it this time, well done! Let us celebrate, let us be grateful.

This year though, the bike recycling facility manager has resigned and a new one promised to email me after another quick visit... And then the coronavirus pandemic hits all of us.

Rule
- We cannot fully control what happens with ourselves, others or our creativity efforts. Be grateful, be kind to ourselves and others, always.

A Refreshing: (Re)learning About Numbers

Now we are back in time where this book began (remember me sitting alone in a lecture theatre?). And this year, I was asked to take on the leadership of a quantitative methods course for first year undergraduates in management. My workplace is worried that students are scoring low in numeracy tests and needs to see improvements on this front, also for accreditation and employability purposes (an emerging set of soft tyrannies). To me this could be another form of creative recycling: reuse some educational content whilst I also introduce a bit of creativity into it to make it more enjoyable for students. I feel anxious.

I call upon another old self: an engineer with an interest in mathematics and problem solving, the one who studied engineering and worked for a bit in developing software. I try to make this challenge exciting for myself and students. I see an opportunity to introduce them to ideas about how the brain 'learns' (Eagleman 2015; Oakley 2014), and *how learning could also be conceived of as creating* (Oakley 2014). I also want to help students who, in my view, had not been adequately taught this course in previous years. Too heavy on the side of advanced statistics, too little on having a gradual learning process.

As one of my previous mentors recommended: 'Rise to the bottom!', meaning that as educators we should assume little knowledge and motivation from our students, something that does not sit very well with my child and perfectionist self, the one who learned maths very quickly and enjoyed this subject until his early twenties.

This situation is a refreshing one, a re-starting one too. I learnt about numbers many years ago. Now it feels like the first time I am doing it.

Currently and outside my work office door there is a board where I have posted a quote from Lehrer (2012, p. 23):

> *When students are given full instructions, when they know exactly what to do, they become easily bored. Curiosity is a fragile thing.*

I feel anxious however: it is a course with over five hundred students! I feel all eyes are on me. Because of this, I start preparations. After a conversation with colleagues (including the previous course leader), I notice that I want to radically transform this course. I feel my shoulders are heavy now.

I re-read Barbara Oakley (2014)'s book. In the early course lectures, I introduce her two modes of brain activity: Diffuse and Focused. I explain that the diffuse mode is a kind of warehouse in which the brain stores ideas and makes connections between those of them which we consider loose or distant from each other. We do so often unconsciously, making use of the hypothalamus and other networks of the brain (Lehrer 2012; Eagleman 2015). The focused mode is when the brain stores ideas in the frontal cortex, to make connections between adjacent elements.

I ask my students to think of three things that they are curious about (Wagner 2015). I get very profound answers: 'afterlife, planetary life, Brexit' are some of their responses. I encourage them to ask themselves these questions when tackling a mathematical problem to generate possibilities: 'What if?' or 'Why not?' (Craft 2013; Barros-Castro et al. 2014). With a few exercises, I show them our brains often trick us by enticing us to jump into the first available answer we find (Dobelli 2013).

I also bring my systems-thinking self as well. I teach my students different types of problem-solving: (a) solving it (finding the best solution); (b) resolving it (finding acceptable solutions); and (c) dissolving it (challenging our assumptions or self-imposed constraints about the problem, imagining novel and systemic ones) (Ackoff 1987).

In this course I think I am putting some of my best individual, creative public selves before students in this private space of the classroom. I play the recorder to help them visualise mathematics and numbers (this felt like a public audition, but I enjoyed it somehow!). I use humour in my examples. I include some bits on the history of mathematics and problem solving. My intention is to generate a sense of wonder, which could help us start articulating (business and management) situations in terms of problems and equations. I tell them to be patient with themselves. Learning takes time and practice.

In some lectures, I also throw a frisbee at some of them with questions about what they are curious about or what they have learned from me so far. In others I ask my students to stand up. I encourage them to shout 'fail!' and clap: I want to include failure as part of their language and celebrate it as a learning opportunity. I can see some of them are a bit confused or curious. There are always those who don't want to stand up or who refuse to do so when I ask them to repeat the exercise.

I show a human side of myself that students would not normally see (Berg and Seeber 2016). For instance, I show my bag contents (including the frisbee), my passion for writing, my desire to do some diffuse thinking and go to a nearby lake and take a walk as a way of ruminating through the ideas that I have about my research projects (my books being some of them) (Oakley, 2014). I try to breathe. I play with the room's lighting. I tell them stories about my children, my previous jobs, life back in Colombia.

I play the recorder at an away meeting with colleagues. I learned to play as a child. Some of my colleagues look surprised. Others clap or encourage me to practice if I want to sound better. I just say: I play to my students to help them better understand maths and have a hobby or go for a walk if they feel tired (Fig. 7.2).

I think in this course we play together with creativity and students. I invite them into my space for individual selves, I show them some of my precious selves and activities. We inhabit the house together. We go back in time and restart our relationship with numbers. We do maths exercises together, we imagine. I challenge their assumptions about education: I say it is likely they have been trained to fear failure and produce the right answers, the ones I want to hear. I humour them. I tell also them to be patient with themselves.

In a more 'serious' tone, I learn to record online lectures and set up online tests for this course on the hoof: everything is set up this way. I talk to colleagues and seek help. It feels like some of my old selves (engineer,

My selves

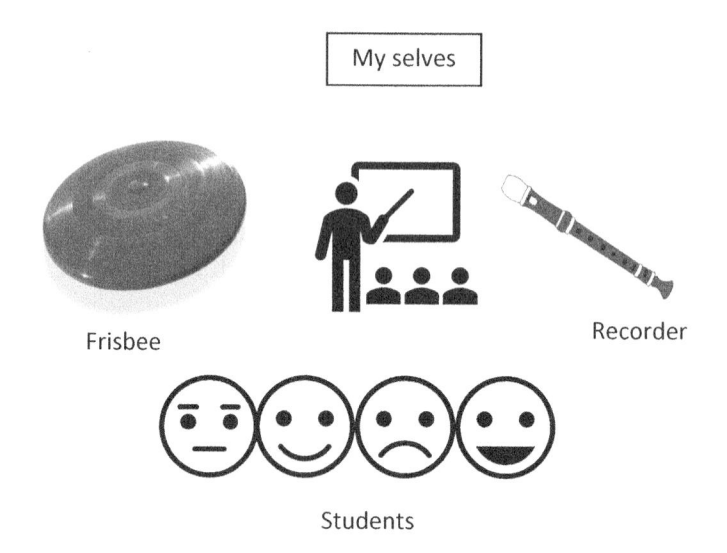

Frisbee   Students   Recorder

Fig. 7.2 (Re)learning about numbers

perfectionist-anxious) are taking over the impending deadlines. It has been many years since learning numbers! And I feel the pressure to do well and do it quickly. I feel all eyes and institutional constraints that make me offer the best experiences to students are on me on the days of the online tests. I also need to be bit more patient with myself. I encourage my team of tutors to value the positives.

Rule
- We could still use our best selves with creativity when we do the things that we value and in the midst of pressures and mis preparations;
- No one is really looking when we are creative 😊; we just need to be bit more patient with ourselves.

Iteration: Did We Fail?

I should (could) have followed the previous rule(s) more to the letter!

In one of the above learning numbers course lectures, some students walk out of the lecture theatre. I later find out that they were not interested in what I was saying. I follow up by email, asking them to be more 'professional' in their attitudes. I get anxious. Soft tyrannies do really shape our roles.

In addition, the online tests don't go smoothly. In the first one, I get called to come to the room where students are taking it. I find out that I made some editing mistakes and that our digital, online learning environment displays graphics or information differently or inaccurately. Faces of some students and invigilator show anxiety. I quickly correct the mistakes and ask students to refresh their screens. The number of mistakes reduces as students and I identify new ones in subsequent test sessions during that day.

It will be several nights of self-worry and self-berating which affect me. My helpful administrators offer some students the opportunity to test again. I meet some of the most concerned to offer reassurances and tell them they did not fail. I also discover a calculation error and remark the whole cohort. I am not allowed to offer detailed feedback on which test questions they got wrong. I send several emails to all students to continue reassuring them that they will be OK.

As I share my feelings and thoughts with colleagues and loved ones, it seems that students and I got caught in a soft tyrannies generated situation, where we exchange blows for what happened in the face of 'blind' feedback: we do not have much time to reflect, listen or talk to each other. Being playful and doing online tests (inherited from someone else) did not sit together easily. We are subjects of these 'governing' technologies, as play could also become the 'norm', to the detriment of seriousness. Any failure is to be managed within this assessment territory, even if its potential causes or consequences reside outside it. I could however, seriously acknowledge 'failure', humour a bit about it, be more mindful, and restart.

This situation has been a refreshing of play: it is now me teaching rather than only learning numbers. I fail, I quickly correct my mistakes. I learn to better use digital assessment technologies. I communicate with students using it. I get anxious. And so, they. I think I just met my match: Perfectionist-anxious students! Some of these students offer good suggestions to improve the assessment though. Grateful, always grateful. Restart.

Rules
- Cover the basics of any assignment or course and do it slowly and gradually. That is also part of being creative.
- Simple exercises will do for the time being when refreshing learning about numbers and in large courses.

- One step at a time please. We cannot please everybody, especially if there are five hundred of them! (Did you hear, perfectionist-anxious selves?)
- We did (not) fail. I say 'we' because failure deserves a systemic analysis beyond assessment.

Iteration: Feedback and (Self) Compassion Arrive

In the above course (learning about numbers), students got good results in the online tests. Some of them tell me they were pleased with my teaching; others get enthusiastic about the potential to further explore how the brain works in further management courses. I feel we (me and my course team) were able to improve things from last year.

Nevertheless, other feedback from student-staff committees was a bit 'different'. I hear and read students' comments like: 'This course is a waste of time'. 'The lecturer is not serious'. 'Neither lecturers nor practice tutors speak clearly'. 'There was not enough practice'. Some of this feedback also arrives via online evaluations, giving us an overall score. Feedback: another governing technology made more immediate, impersonal, sophisticated, punishing to a great extent.

Following Drummond (2013), I try to interpret feedback. I could have been focused on my own mathematics-knowledgeable/playful self, to the potential detriment of other ones (organised, helpful, hard-working and serious) or the students' (worried, hateful of numbers, assertive, anxious-perfectionist, careless, demanding) ones. Nevertheless,

> *When reading the feedback, my friend creativity says, in a playful/serious way:*
> *"So, what did you expect? Why so many students (500)? Why such late teaching hours?*
> *Why did you keep anxiously checking up on me and students?*
> *To be fair, you did what you could, and some of your lectures also went over my head* 😊 *!"*

My first reactions to the above student feedback suggest that myself, I am taking all responsibility for it, am being too harsh on myself; I acknowledge this when meditating and with the help of others. Perhaps because I wanted things to be perfect, or perhaps because I drained myself in the attempt to please students' (perhaps unrealistic) expectations, I was not able to fully appreciate it, doubting that 'good' feedback was true. Within soft tyrannies, not many people beside my selves want to hear about failure, let alone share responsibilities for it or success.

Interestingly, I also got an email from a student's partner from another country who heard about my playfulness and some of the negative reactions I received and encouraged me to continue instilling creativity in my courses and my students. 'We need tutors like you', he would say.

Rules (Thanks to My Friend John)
- There is always room for improvement if not learning in everything we think or do as human beings.
- Let us play to be compassionate, let us try to appreciate ourselves and others more fully. Let us try to find humour in all this.

Time for self-recovery balms: stop, rest, seek support, talk about my feelings, watch movies, organise things, play with daughter Sofia to remind myself that we can always forget and start again. Her games, her rules, possibly the same with my students. Let us all be who we are now, let us accept ourselves bit more.

Rules
- There could be emotional support around to help us deal with failures (wife, well-being groups, close friends).

In a more compassionate and serious manner, student feedback could be reinterpreted as another, emerging **governing technology** which, alongside play and assessment, aims to ensure that both educators and students assume certain conducts and achieve governing objectives laid out by governing programmes like the ones laid out earlier in this book. On this occasion, mediated by ICT and 'like a bull in a china shop', feedback has entered the space created for individual selves: we left the door open, and the bull had a field day.

I forgot that my teaching team and students' freedom is framed within soft tyrannies power. We got too close to our collectively defined boundaries. As perfectionist-anxious selves, we can really harm or be harmed by using this sort of technology; we could be reinforcing it with ICT mediated ones.

We all need to stop, become silent, and if possible, better articulate what we think is going on; consider the existence of other selves whose feedback could protect creativity and us.

We could consider other governing technologies to enable mistakes to be corrected without affecting creativity or education. Maybe we just need to express how we feel as a way of protecting ourselves and others and with the possibility of creating better instances for reflection, dialogue or participation within soft tyrannies.

And try to become less serious, more compassionate with ourselves and others.

Feedback Rules
- When being 'feedback tasered' by soft tyrannies in management education, it is better to stop, be silent, reflect, self-soothe, laugh about it, speak with others, and later, if needed, speak up. Creativity wants us to be compassionate and realistic with what we can achieve within tyrannies.

Time to Stop, Reflect and Be Serious Again

Soft tyrannies: Stop! You are ruining learning for all of us! Refresh, re-start.

Within this game of selves protection, being serious would mean suspending judgement about ourselves as educators; restore perceived imbalances between collective and individual roles in management education, restraining or arguing against the effects that governing technologies like feedback is having on all of us.

This is what creativity and I have to say to be more self-compassionate. **We need to say no to** large lecture theatres, doubling up teaching, standardising learning, fully automating online assessment. These and other things make us educators and students more anxious. They make us become or adopt more perfectionist and anxious selves, isolated, unhappy selves. Time to stop and reflect before taking any further action.

Cup of tea?

So, what really happened? Perhaps we will never fully find out, and that should be OK.

A Final, Ethical Rule
- This is what I have to say to myself, other educators and students: Let us try to be or become more compassionate, ok or good enough selves in education and beyond.

Concluding Reflections

This chapter has narrated my experiences of engaging with creativity at present. Such experiences have revealed several different selves that have surfaced with the help of ideas previously presented. In the space for nurturing creativity that was carved out previously in this book, these selves have mostly performed a collective role of educating others.

Through several refreshing(s) and iterations of the game I call 'let us protect our most precious, private selves', and using ideas about nurturing creativity in education previously explored in this book, I have been able to advance creativity; as a friend, creativity has been there to help convey ideas about recycling, cycling and learning about numbers. I have also been able to show some of my most precious selves to students.

Playing this new game has also allowed me to elicit several useful rules. These suggest that we should keep safe emotionally and mentally; use creativity to tackle real world problems from our physical surroundings; ensure that we also keep our imagination going so that we can entice our students to experience wonder and surprise; celebrate successes when our students make sense of creativity; accept failure as a systemic issue that involves us and others, be more understanding and tolerant, cover gradually the basics of domains of knowledge, and use feedback to promote self-compassion in ourselves and students, even if that means saying 'no' or 'back off!' to existing and potentially detrimental educational practices in management.

There could be times where we need to become **silent or serious** about creativity, meaning that we need to protect ourselves and our students by using feedback to promote systemic changes that are needed in our management educational systems. Being creative also means being able to shift and share responsibility for 'failure' to such systems as a way of living an ethos towards our present time(s).

(Self) counter-conducts can also be about pushing back; redesigning governing programmes (mass education) or technologies (i.e. online feedback and assessment), and reacting against what we see as negative effects of power technologies and emerging functions. In my case, taking on large management courses and expecting 'positive' if not 'perfect' student feedback could be twofold: as my own fault as educator (I needed to cover the basics bit better, although I think I did an OK job, all things considered), but also as a systemic fault of a system that does not ask itself if these practices are good for us all.

For this reason, there need to be creativity opportunities to design educational environments that do not take their toll on educators or students. It is time to rethink what management education wants to achieve and how it wants to achieve it.

The infusion of creativity could not be only seen as a way of reinforcing existing and limited conceptions about who educators or students are or should be (cogs in an increasingly sophisticated operating machinery that serves economic and knowledge demands). Rather, creativity in education could be also seen as an opportunity to go back to our most precious selves, manage and protect them from increasing governing programmes and economies of scale, many of which are currently being reinforced by the use of digital technologies.

The insights of this chapter could lead to small, silent but powerful reflections which could trigger individual and systemic actions in management education. As educators, let us keep playing and being serious. There is still freedom and time to do so. And in between our playfulness and seriousness, we could become ok or good enough people for our own benefit and future, and that of others around us.

References

Ackoff, R. L. (1987). *The Art of Problem Solving – Accompanied by Ackoff's Fables*. New York: John Wiley and Sons. New edition.

Barros-Castro, R., Córdoba-Pachón, J. R., & Pinzón-Salcedo, L. (2014). A Systemic Framework for Evaluating Computer-Supported Collaborative Learning—Mathematical Problem-solving (CSCL-MPS) Initiatives: Insights from a Colombian Case. *Systemic Practice and Action Research, 27*, 265–285.

Bateson, M. C. (1994). *Peripheral Visions: Learning Along the Way*. New York: Harper.

Berg, M., & Seeber, B. (2016). *The Slow Professor: Challenging the Culture of Speed in the Academy*. Toronto: University of Toronto Press.

Córdoba-Pachón, J. R., Campbell, T. (2008). Learning to deal with CSR issues in the classroom. *Systems Research and Behavioral Science, 25*(3), 427–437.

Clapp, E. (2017). *Participatory Creativity: Introducing Access to Equity to the Creative Classroom*. New York: Routledge.

Córdoba-Pachón, J. R. (2019). *Managing Creativity: A Systems Thinking Journey*. London: Routledge.

Craft, A. (2013). Childhood, Possibility Thinking and Wise, Humanising Educational Future. *International Journal of Educational Research, 61*, 126–134.

Cropley, D., & Cropley, A. (2016). Promoting Creativity Through Assessment: A Formative Computer-Assisted Assessment Tool for Teachers. *Educational Technology, 56*(6), 17–24.

Dobelli, R. (2013). *The Art of Thinking Clearly.* London: Sceptre.

Droit, J. P. (2018). *Volver a ser Niño: Experiencias de Filosofía* (trans: Núria Petit Fontserè). Spain: Ediciones Paidós.

Drummond, J. (2013). Care of the Self in a Knowledge Economy: Higher education, vocation and the ethics of Michel Foucault. *Educational Philosophy and Theory, 35*(3), 57–69.

Eagleman, D. (2015). *The Brain: The Story of You.* London: Canongate.

Lehrer, J. (2012). *Imagine: How Creativity Works.* New York: Houghton Mifflin Harcourt.

Montuori, A. (2012). Creative Inquiry: Confronting the Challenges of Scholarship in the 21st Century. *Futures, 44,* 64–70.

Oakley, B. (2014). *A Mind for Numbers.* New York: Tarcher/Putnam.

Wagner, T. (2015). *Creating Innovators: The Making of Young People Who Will Change the World.* New York: Scribner, Simon and Schuster, Inc.

Wright, R. (2017). *Why Buddhism Is True – The Science and Philosophy of Meditation and Enlightenment.* New York: Simon and Schuster.

CHAPTER 8

Summaries, Implications and Epilogue

Introduction

This chapter presents two summaries of the book. First, the argument is revisited. Then, key insights are conveyed together in a summary of the argument, potential implications for the rediscovery of creativity in management education, and a guide of how to play a game called rediscovering creativity in management education. Finally, an epilogue.

The Argument Revisited

This book has developed a critical stance about creativity in management education, one which aims to inspire educators, students and other people interested in taking a step back, and venturing to reflect and act on what it means to rediscover creativity.

The stance has been developed by first providing an analysis of the operation of soft tyrannies in management education. This analysis, inspired by Foucault's governmentality ideas, has shown how a sophisticated set of discourses and practices has contributed to narrow down 'other' options to be or learn to be creative than those contributing to economic growth or the disciplining of creativity as a body of knowledge. From this initial reflection, several counter-conduct possibilities were proposed. In pursuing them, a further review of current efforts to nurture creativity was undertaken.

There are several initiatives that currently nurture creativity, many of which could be reflected upon or adopted for management education. From encouraging people to pursue their inner passions and interests to setting up adequate learning, environmental or communication conditions to help them do so, in many of the initiatives the activity of play is also encouraged. A systemic paradox for individual selves was identified: we are encouraged to use our 'inner' energy to become part of 'wholes' (educational systems, organisations) whilst already being valued as members of these. We are to 'self-develop' or 'grow' to be 'fully accepted' within these wholes, nurturing our creativity to do so. To address the above paradox, a further exploration of Foucault's ideas on governmentality is made. A systemic space for thinking and acting, now at a more micro (individual) level of governmentality, is proposed, one which is directed to governing ourselves, rather than being fully governed by soft tyrannies.

For our present time(s), Foucault's proposed attitude to the Enlightenment era reveals that it is possible, if not essential, for people to assume different selves, and do so individually or collectively via roles and practices. With this attitude, enquirers can also become educators. We could become/show someone else (different selves including our old and precious ones), using practices like learning, writing or meditating, or doing them in a humorous way. A systemic space for selves could become a 'house' we can inhabit with creativity through roles and practices, whichever type of definition(s) we attribute to these companions.

A spirit of play (and seriousness) is also introduced to help individual selves inhabit the space previously proposed with creativity: a first start every time, where we try to articulate and set rules for how the space is to be inhabited, a continuous refresh or restart. Spiriting play and seriousness can help us iterate, refresh, articulate or even ground ourselves in realities made visible by soft tyrannies in management education. These and other practices, as well as different roles (individual, collective) for selves, could lead us to conceive of our lives as 'games' with norms, rules and improvisations. We can stop playing them to reflect, possibly adopt more 'serious' attitudes, reformulate rules or engage in other games we could define. Play/seriousness, their imbalance, could lead us to adopt a more palatable paradox to nurture creativity in ourselves and others in management education.

Further Implications for the Rediscovery of Creativity

There are several important implications derived from considering the above and narrated games in our current reality in management education, which could be used to revisit the (self) counter-conduct possibilities laid out in Chap. 2 of this book.

Firstly, I have revealed myself as an individual and public subject, one which has guessed where the muse of creativity has been or is in my life. I have revealed different and valuable selves, moving also from the individual to the collective and back, using practices like reading, writing, reflecting, mindfulness meditation, socialising, humouring or the support from others to engage with creativity and keep it alive.

Creativity, a muse, then a friend, now a partner (see epilogue later on in this chapter) with my different selves has been there playing key games. With the derived games' rules, we have been able to identify limits and possibilities together. These limits and possibilities suggest that we need not to entirely abandon who we have been or are, but rather let our different selves flourish. We need not stick to one conception of creativity or who we are, but rather to adopt several which we could use to better help ourselves and others.

And we need to keep smiling or laughing about things, even on the face of perceived and serious success or failure. *These impostors...*

Secondly, by revealing my selves through the pursuit of creativity in its different forms, it has also been possible to reveal other features of soft tyrannies in management education. These mostly operate silently when it comes to letting us deal with the systemic paradox identified for creativity in education (it is me doing all the articulating and reflecting!). They could easily bring a perfectionist idea of who we are to become as creative subjects, reinforcing it with sophisticated and ICT technologies like student assessment and feedback (and now online teaching due to coronavirus and its aftermath). They leave us with the responsibility for nurturing creativity(ies) whilst they become better at perfecting the already perfect, which could often result in appropriations to suit short-term (economic, scale) needs to the potential detriment of better communications or reflections between ourselves and others.

And thirdly, soft tyrannies for management education could be currently reaching a threshold or status of self-producing technologies of government (Dean 1996). What this means is that soft tyrannies have started to offer glimpses of self-serving. Increasingly blind to or detached from 'other' governing programmes (better attention to students' diversity), convergences of technologies of feedback and assessment could be increasing their focus on defining and correcting deviations from their own norms and rules. Like a big game that we are to inevitably play, soft tyrannies could then seek better standardisation, (ICT-based) assessment or better economies of scale, more 'normal' students with fewer educators or resources, less time to reflect, less creativity, less humanly oriented management education.

To these implications, the emerging rules and the space proposed in this book could help us continue devising ways to counteract the negative effects of tyrannies' emerging functions. One of them could be to *bring creativity and education to selves* rather than the other way around, to devise governing programmes and technologies that reflect this, and do so in more compassionate ways for us all.

As educators in management, we could also carve out opportunities for (self) reflection whilst we keep the more and digital/ICT-mediated efficiency-focused ones at bay (i.e. we could humourously or graciously say no to them!); we could continue critically identifying and denouncing their power relations and their effects. We could let or continue letting ourselves and students express their creativities in different ways. We could explore other ways to fail or promote failure safely and meaningfully in ourselves, our junior educator colleagues and our students (Córdoba-Pachón et al, 2020). We could also cultivate our solitary and individual ways of being.

Moreover, there could be another possibility to become playful/serious about what goes on. We could remain silent or say no with a smile. We could also with a smile, become **uncreative**. This at times would need to be done for our own sake or sanity. But always in mind that at some point our most precious selves would like to seek and find creativity, engaging with individual or collective roles to do so in our societies, as if we were living more fully our lives. We could always have time to stop and reflect before deciding what to do or be next.

And a last rule for the reader, extended from musical songs and what has been ruled before from the games' narratives:

8 SUMMARIES, IMPLICATIONS AND EPILOGUE

- 'Nobody said rediscovering creativity was easy. But so is life, our lives. Always be grateful for both your creativity and our lives. Let us restart/refresh, let us keep going, let us do so for our own sakes and those of our students'.

It might not be easy to start following this and the other and emerging rules in this book to rediscover creativity, let alone to continue. We should at least try and restart, keep going …Creativity is on our side.

A Brief Summary Guide to Play 'Rediscovering Creativity in Management Education'

Students: You are (re) entering an environment where you are attracted by an ideal of learning with others (including people like me as educators).

On arrival, make sure you understand what your institution(s) have been and where they want to go. Some of them might pay lip service to nurturing your creativity. Spend time selecting the best place where your different selves have a greater chance of flourishing, not only getting a good job at the end. Enjoy, be grateful, restart, laugh. Take and do not take things too seriously.

During your visits as a student: obey, do your homework, do not expect miracles without some good work. Instead, expect some possibilities to reflect on who you have been, who you are or want to be. They will occur in the least expected places though. Keep your eyes open.

Take some risks, not every time. If you think is a good idea, accept invitations to venture in alleyways; self-protect but also nurture your talents, imagination and curiosity.

Caution You need to protect your best selves from becoming too (un) 'creative' according to institutional views of what it means to teach creativity, teaching creatively or becoming creative. You can always exert your creativity in different, unexpected ways.

To deal with the above caution, make sure you find someone like a mentor or good friends. Remember that all of us could be trying to protect ourselves from becoming too (un) 'creative'. The more playful she or your other friends are, the better so that you can all keep smiling whilst also being serious or even mystical about life. And also remember that there could be limits to playfulness.

And the pandemic? Let us try to imagine new forms of compassionate interaction. Let us try to see what and who is behind the screen.

Be grateful for your visit(s) and for the people who have made them possible. There will be great and hard times, they are all opportunities to learn about your different selves and those of other people.

And when you finish or decide to finish your studies, I wish you all the best. Remember, life is very precious. Stay safe and sane. Be grateful. Restart, refresh.

Educators: If you are still thinking about creativity or doing something about it, it means you cannot live without it, despite your and my best efforts.

You want to rediscover creativity? First, you need to be willing to bring some of your 'old' selves (individual, collective) and things you used to love back to the present.

Second, you need to find or create a space for your different selves and your creativities, whatever definitions you have of the latter. The space could be a course, a workshop, a meeting with students, a video conference. Soft tyrannies still offer some of these spaces. Keep your eyes open.

Third, in such a space or spaces, prepare learning activities with simple rules. We are to pretend we are not who we are supposed to be or do. That takes some courage and optimism, bit of bending of norms, improvisation and a smile.

Some examples of activities: together with students and creativity, we are going to explore the basics of a subject, we are going to recycle, we are going to visit an organisation. To those, make sure you know and teach the basics of your topics, and playfully/seriously challenge or go beyond some of the established conventions and boundaries about them.

Let us connect with others from inside or outside and encourage our students to do the same.

Students and others might be asking: and the pandemic? Let us try to imagine new forms of compassionate interaction that go beyond our screens. There will be times to be playful and serious. Let us keep our curiosity, compassion and assertiveness open and together.

Educators: Who said that we cannot break the silos of knowledge? Who said for example that we cannot talk about maths and music together, recycling and digital innovation, recycling process management and social enterprising?

Fourth. We are to improvise, humour, tease, smile, laugh or cry. We are to tell our students that we also fail, and we will try to correct mistakes as soon as possible. We are to let them know we are there for them as mentors if they think we can help them rediscover themselves. We are to act on failure, but not take all the blame for it. There are soft tyrannies behind whatever we do. Let other people play their part, in the good and not so good of management education.

Fifth. We are also to be serious or even uncreative in this game. Whether we are conscious of it or no, we are to be somehow mentors of our students. We are to receive feedback from all sides (good, bad) which we will find difficult to swallow. Let us take time to digest feedback. Let us sit on it whilst we decide what is best for all of us.

Sixth. Let's not ignore these or the use of ICTs in education, their opening and constraining potential. Let us look at them beyond monitoring or assessment, and with an eye of (self) compassion and better understanding.

Seventh. We are to make sure we continue educating by engaging, not only instructing or assessing ourselves or others.

Let us play. Let us listen, let us observe, let us slow down, let us talk, let us keep going. Let us look for and support companions and people who cheer you up on the way. Let us make our own well-being a priority.

Let us continue playing. Let us be patient with ourselves and others. It might take some time and sweat to (re) create or defend ourselves and our creativities from soft tyrannies. But every small step, failure or achievement will be worth it. Let us celebrate creativity, let us be serious and grateful, always.

Educators and Students: Let us accept we cannot play this game as lonely figures. There are still possibilities to exert our freedom and become (more) creative within them.

Other Game Participants: This game cannot be played without your direct or indirect participation.

One only instruction please. Let us not take the other games you are playing (more students, larger cohorts, more assessment, more economies of scale, rearing successful children, world-famous research) too playfully/seriously please.

Otherwise, where are the fun, the pain and the joy of educating? Or living?

I know other educator colleagues, or you also might be asking: And the pandemic? My answer is, let us continue imagining and designing new forms of compassionate interaction. Our world has changed, and so could we. Let us be grateful, always.

And an Epilogue

On our honeymoon and shortly after our wedding, creativity and I toured around. We arrived in Colombia where things were open but formal: students there are like me, perfectionist-anxious, hardworking and open to learning. The Ricardos and the Luises.

On our way back to Europe, we stopped in Spain to work on different uses of plastic cups with students. We met great characters there and our host Teresa was wary of creativity being packaged in engineering and business education. We met some engineering students who said they would be happier by practising what they were learning.

We then went to France where they said creativity was a process, and that I should make my ideas more digestible and practical for audiences like them (information systems and corporate social responsibility educators). One of the attendees to our presentation kindly suggested I should investigate how institutional structures were a key influencer of creativity in individuals. I kindly replied they are funny settings where knowledge is continuously borrowed.

We then went to the North of England to visit old friends of mine (Amanda, Gerald). I was asked for specific definitions of creativity by Mike. Somehow, I was forced to concede that in order to become creative, one has first to know something about something, and that I could be rejected if sending my writing to creativity or systems thinking journals. I said to him that I wrote my books without an idea to convert them into journal articles. I just wrote them. I found a good voice. I was sweating when answering his questions. Then, I stopped playing and reflected, finding that there was another game I did not want to play.

Still, I sometimes have my doubts. Has this journey really been about creativity rediscovery *or simply an ego-driven typewriting and surviving/politicking effort?*

Another visit to a friend on our way home left me thinking that I already had a path to follow: to continue promoting creativity in my courses and to accept responsibility for the consequences, being more self-compassionate. And since coming home I can hear creativity saying, with a calmed voice:

> My dearest, welcome to married life. I chose you because of who you are when you write and when you despair or smile. I love your curiosity, when you write your notes and your books that neither I nor close family (or students!) understand. And that is OK.
>
> Count your blessings. Listen, pay attention and observe; mindfully meditate. Work on your perfectionism and anxieties. Be kind to yourself and others. Let us be all safe.
>
> And let us restart, let us keep going, always grateful!

May 2020

References

Córdoba-Pachón, J. R., Mapelli, J. R., Al Taji, F., & Donovan, D. (2020). Systemic creativities in sustainability and social innovation education. *Systemic Practice and Action Research, forthcoming.* https://doi.org/10.1007/s11213-020-09530-z, accessed July 2020.

Dean, M. (1996). Putting the Technological into Government. *History of the Human Sciences, 9*(3), 47–68.

Index

A
Agents, 31, 51
Alleyway, 78–80
Anxiety, 22, 31, 64, 77, 81, 84, 86, 103
Attention, 2, 15, 35, 37, 40, 41, 87, 114

B
Buddhism, 52

C
Cemeteries, 49
Classroom, 93–108
Collaboration, 4, 33, 39, 49
Colombia, xiii, 2, 84, 85, 101, 118
Conduct, 6, 12–14, 17, 21, 23, 24, 30, 53, 54, 57, 111
Coronavirus, 15, 20, 96, 97, 99, 113
Corporate social responsibility, 118
Creative subject, 5, 6, 8, 11, 12, 18–21, 23, 24, 29, 33, 53, 55–57, 113
  creative-productive, 55

Creativity, vii, xiv, 1, 2, 4–8, 11–24, 29–44, 47–53, 56–58, 63, 64, 66–74, 77–91, 93–108, 111–115, 118, 119
  abilities or traits, 19
  assessment frameworks, 19
  assessments, 23, 41, 64
  categorisation, 17, 23
  cognitive processes, 19, 31, 51
  definitions, 12
  domains of knowledge, 11, 19
  generic criteria, 16
  individual tests, 16
  initiatives, 29, 30, 43, 112
  inner energy, 31, 35, 42, 44, 58
  lineages, 48
  muse, 7, 36, 77, 91, 93, 113
  nurturing, 1, 2, 5, 6, 16, 19, 20, 24, 29, 30, 32, 33, 40–44, 47, 53, 56–58, 66, 69, 107, 111–113
  qualities, 12, 20
  rediscovery, 8, 12, 24, 30, 47, 49, 91, 111, 113–115
  research, 16
  socio-cultural, 16, 49, 58, 66
  teaching learning, 17

D
Design thinking, 18, 98
Diffusion, 37, 38

E
Education, 2–4, 6, 11, 15, 17, 19, 21, 23, 24, 29–35, 39–44, 49, 50, 53, 54, 56, 57, 65–67, 69, 72, 78, 84, 85, 89, 105–108, 112, 113, 118
  engineering education, 1, 2, 6, 41, 80, 84–86, 118
Educational institutions, 49, 86, 90, 91
Educational systems, 6, 8, 12, 22, 23, 42, 50, 52, 65, 107, 112
Educators, xiv, 1–8, 11, 12, 19–23, 29–32, 35, 36, 41, 42, 53, 55, 56, 65–67, 82, 91, 98–100, 105–108, 111, 112, 114, 118
Entrepreneurial, 3
Ethics, 2, 11, 15, 50, 51, 56, 57, 66
  ethos, 54, 56, 107
  principles, 49, 54, 57, 69, 70

F
Failure, 7, 19, 21, 31, 32, 34, 49, 71, 77, 89, 101, 107, 114
  failing, 4, 19, 35, 39
Father of twins, 35
Feedback, 7, 98, 103–107, 113
Foucault, Michel, 5, 6, 11, 12, 15, 17, 20, 21, 23, 24, 44, 47, 48, 53–58, 72, 111, 112
Freedom, 5, 14, 20, 22, 23, 29, 54, 55, 58, 85, 105
Free individuals, 11

G
Game, 6, 7, 35, 37, 39, 63, 64, 66, 68–70, 72, 73, 77–79, 83, 88–90, 93–96, 98, 107, 112–114

Governing programmes, 15, 17, 18, 20, 34, 47, 57, 105, 107, 108, 114
  Creativity Disciplining, 16–17
  discourses, 23, 54, 55, 111
  Education for Economic Growth, 15–16
Governing technologies, 17, 23, 42, 57, 105, 106
  assessment, 19, 21, 23, 41, 55, 57, 66, 91, 97, 105–107, 114
  assessment technologies, 19
  standardisation, 17, 19, 23, 31, 41, 42, 55, 57, 114
Government, 15, 17, 53, 114
Governmentality, 5, 6, 11, 12, 24, 43, 44, 47, 48, 53, 54, 56–58, 72, 94, 111, 112

H
Humanism, 54

I
Idea biography, 49, 71–72
Information and communication technologies (ICTs), 20, 53, 65, 66, 89, 103
Innovation, 11, 16, 21, 32–34, 43, 63, 68, 97–98
Introvert, 4, 64

L
Lack of time, 2, 20–22, 57, 64, 95, 96, 98
Learning, 1, 6, 7, 18–23, 34, 35, 37–41, 44, 54, 57, 58, 63–67, 78, 79, 86, 89–91, 94–96, 99–107, 112, 118
  success, 32, 39, 49, 85
  systemic idea of, 40
Life stories, 71
Lump, 82–83

M

Management education, xiv, 3–8, 11–24, 29, 30, 34, 43, 44, 48, 49, 53, 55–58, 63–65, 71, 73, 93, 94, 106, 108, 111–113
Mathematics, 3, 41, 99, 101, 104
Mentors, 19, 32, 33, 84, 87, 90, 100
Mindfulness meditation, 7, 22, 55, 78, 89, 95, 113
  meditating, 57, 58, 78, 112
Moral growth/development
  morally grow, 18
Mystical, 55, 56, 94

N

Narratives, 5, 49, 51, 54, 68, 72, 73, 77, 78, 90, 93
Numeracy skills, 3
Nurturing creativity, 29, 43, 56, 107, 113

O

Oriental, 55

P

Perfectionist-anxious, 1, 80–83, 85, 87–91, 93, 95, 96, 98, 102, 104, 105, 118
Philosophy, 1, 50, 54
Play, 4–7, 30, 32–36, 39, 41, 42, 47, 50, 58, 63–73, 77, 80, 81, 83, 89, 90, 93, 94, 96–98, 101, 103, 105, 112, 114
Power, 5, 6, 11, 12, 14–17, 20–23, 32, 40, 47, 54, 55, 57, 66, 72, 96, 105, 107, 114
  emerging power functions, 14, 20–22
Practically oriented learning, 4
Practice, xiv, 1, 5–7, 12, 15, 18–19, 21, 23, 33, 38, 41–43, 47–49, 51, 55–58, 63, 65, 67, 69–71, 73, 77, 78, 81, 88, 90, 91, 93, 96, 97, 101, 104, 107, 111–113
Public, 47, 54, 84, 85, 87, 88, 101

R

Reading, 7, 22, 55, 65, 77–79, 81, 86, 88, 90, 104, 113
Recycling, 94–99, 107
Reflect, 1, 4, 5, 7, 8, 11, 19, 32, 36, 42, 55, 64, 69, 78, 89, 106, 111, 112, 114
Reflection, 65
  individual solitude and reflection, 22
  solitary or individual, 65
Relaxation, 37
Roles, 6, 7, 19, 31, 40, 42, 43, 47–49, 51, 56–58, 63, 67, 69–71, 73, 77, 90, 106, 112, 114
Rule, 6, 7, 64, 66–70, 72–74, 78, 80–89, 91, 93, 96–99, 102, 103, 105–107, 112–114

S

Saying no, 22, 94, 107
Schools, 15, 36, 39–42, 85
Self, 4–6, 12, 17–19, 21, 23, 24, 30, 31, 37–40, 42, 43, 47–58, 65, 67, 70, 80, 81, 83, 85, 86, 88–90, 93–96, 98–100, 103–107, 114
  compassion, 42, 89, 104–107
Self-determination, 30, 31
Self-development/efficacy, 18
Self-efficacy, 31
Selves, 1, 4, 6, 7, 12, 15, 16, 24, 30, 32, 36, 37, 39, 40, 42–44, 47, 49–55, 57–58, 63–65, 67, 69, 70, 72, 73, 77, 78, 81, 83, 87–91, 93–95, 97, 101, 102, 104–108, 112–114
  fluid, 40, 48, 51, 53

Serious, 5, 22, 52, 56, 66, 70–73, 78, 83, 88–91, 93, 94, 104, 106–108, 112, 114
Soft tyrannies, 5–8, 12, 14, 29, 32, 39, 41–43, 48, 52, 53, 55–58, 63, 65, 73, 86, 89–91, 93, 95, 99, 105, 106, 111–114
Spirit, 5–7, 58, 63, 64, 67–73, 77, 78, 80, 83, 87, 89, 94, 97, 112
Spirit of play (and seriousness), 7
  objects, 68, 69, 77, 78, 93
  seriousness, 6, 7, 42, 64, 65, 69–73, 78, 83, 87, 89, 96, 108, 112
  spirit of childhood, 7, 64, 67, 68, 70
Students, vii, xiii, 1, 3–7, 12, 15, 21–23, 29, 31, 32, 38, 39, 41, 42, 49, 55, 64, 72, 83, 85, 86, 88, 91, 94–108, 111, 114, 115, 118, 119
Systemic paradox, 6, 29, 43, 44, 47, 50, 53, 57, 70, 112, 113
Systemic rediscovery, 6, 8
Systemic space, 7, 43, 47, 57–58, 112
Systems thinking, xiii, 1, 2, 4–6, 8, 15, 21, 22, 31, 39–42, 47–53, 71, 78, 80, 84–86, 100, 107, 118
systemic, xiv, 6–8, 19, 29, 32, 40, 43, 44, 47–51, 57–58, 89, 94, 100, 107, 108, 112, 113

T
Teachers, 32–34, 79, 86
Teaching, 22
Tutors, 19, 104, 105
Typewrite, 81
Typewriter, 78, 80–82, 84

U
University, vii, xiii, 2, 22, 64, 74, 80, 83–88, 97
University curricula, 2

W
Well-being, 22, 49, 89, 90, 96, 105
Wholes, 29, 40, 44, 49, 52, 54, 57, 70, 112
Writing, 7, 22, 37, 55, 57, 58, 65, 66, 77–82, 87, 88, 90, 101, 112, 113, 118

CPI Antony Rowe
Eastbourne, UK
August 10, 2020